Advance Praise for
Align Your Mind

"Britt Frank is a great storyteller. In this new book she uses her own story of recovery from the depths as well as the stories of many of her clients to inspire you to change your relationship with your parts. I am honored that this accomplished writer and speaker bases much of the book on Internal Family Systems (IFS), the paradigm shift that I am trying to bring to the world. She has found a way to combine IFS with other approaches to create practical exercises for you to not only learn to love parts you've hated, like the inner critic, but help them transform into inner helpers."

—Dr. Richard C. Schwartz, PhD, creator of Internal Family Systems and adjunct faculty at Harvard Medical School

"When your worries get the best of you, pick up this book! This is the most practical book on how to regain your self-efficacy and sanity that I have ever read. Britt Frank's insights are uniquely creative and straightforward to apply. This is not your usual self-help book but a masterpiece of theory, memoir, and clear instruction, complete with thought-provoking quotes from a wide range of sources. Every sentence feels original and has been honed to the point of being therapeutic just through reading it. Do your life a favor and get this profound book. It's written with expert knowledge yet offered in the spirit of the safest friendship you could ever experience."

—Lindsay C. Gibson, PsyD, clinical psychologist and *New York Times* bestselling author of *Adult Children of Emotionally Immature Parents*

"Britt Frank's *Align Your Mind* is a masterclass in self-discovery, delivered with her signature wit and wisdom. Brilliant, funny, and genuinely amazing, Britt has a way of breaking down complex topics with ease, helping you unlock a deeper understanding of yourself while keeping you entertained. A must-read for anyone ready to align their mind and transform their life."

—Mark Groves, founder of Create the Love, host of *The Mark Groves Podcast*, speaker, and coauthor of *Liberated Love*

"In *Align Your Mind*, Britt offers simple yet effective strategies to help you break free from old habits, gain a deeper understanding of your emotions, and transform the harsh voice of your inner critic into a supportive inner coach."

—Jessica Baum, LMHC, author of *Anxiously Attached*

"Britt Frank's *Align Your Mind* reveals that inner peace comes from harmonizing your inner voices, not silencing them. With humor, compassion, and practical tools, Britt makes self-discovery approachable, helping you embrace every part of yourself and live with greater ease."

—Dr. Ellen Vora, psychiatrist and author of *The Anatomy of Anxiety*

"Britt's voice is a lovable burst of new insight and relatable profundity. Her grasp on modern human predicaments will make you feel like she's been reading your mind. If you feel stuck and at war with yourself, wrestle with inner critics, or long to feel free without having to move to a monastery, pick this book up. It's a fun ride dripping with life-changing wisdom."

—Ralph De La Rosa, LCSW, author of *Outshining Trauma: A New Vision of Radical Self-Compassion*

"This book is a masterclass in taming anxiety and healing trauma. Britt Frank's relatable and empowering approach to parts work makes navigating your inner world accessible, engaging, and life-changing."

—Terri Cole, licensed psychotherapist and author of *Boundary Boss*

"Britt Frank is the educated-but-accessible, soothing-but-rousing voice our anxious culture so urgently needs. In a world where the clinical often feels cynical while self-help books can go overboard on hashtag fauxspiration, Frank's wisdom strikes a wonderful balance I dare readers not to enjoy."

—Amanda Montell, *New York Times* bestselling author of *The Age of Magical Overthinking* and *Cultish*

"For years, I have allowed my inner critic to dominate my thoughts, leading to countless episodes of self-injury and emotional turmoil. Britt's approach to parts work gave me the tools to reframe my inner dialogue and harness its power for good. This book is a game-changer for anyone who has ever felt overwhelmed by their own mind."

—Chris Schembra, *Wall Street Journal* bestselling author of *Gratitude Through Hard Times* and *Gratitude and Pasta*

"I truly, honestly, deeply loved every part of Britt Frank's fun, witty, accessible, and incredibly actionable manual for getting the most out of parts work. *Align Your Mind* is part plain-English summary of the last century of neuroscience, part debunking of the last fifty years of awful (but well-meaning) self-help literature, and part collection of deeply honest and practical advice that can only come from someone with decades of therapeutic experience and expertise."

—David McRaney, author of *How Minds Change* and *You Are Not So Smart*

"This is the ultimate guide to parts work. If you want to make sense of your inner world and find a way to feel more at home inside, this book is for you. Britt will show you how to discover the hidden gems inside of you, and how to reconnect with parts of yourself who you may have learned to dislike. With *Align Your Mind*, you'll have the tools to move forward with clarity and purpose."

—Amber Rae, international bestselling author of *Choose Wonder Over Worry* and *The Answers Are Within You*

Align Your Mind

Align
Your Mind

Tame Your Inner Critic
and Make Peace with Your Shadow
Using the Power of Parts Work

Britt Frank, LSCSW

Tarcher
an imprint of Penguin Random House
New York

Tarcher

an imprint of Penguin Random House LLC
1745 Broadway, New York, NY 10019
penguinrandomhouse.com

Tarcher is a registered trademark of Penguin
Random House LLC, and Tarcher with leaf design
is a trademark of Penguin Random House LLC.

Most Tarcher books are available at special quantity discounts for bulk
purchase for sales promotions, premiums, fund-raising, and educational
needs. Special books or book excerpts also can be created to fit specific
needs. For details, write: SpecialMarkets@penguinrandomhouse.com.

Library of Congress Cataloging-in-Publication Data
Names: Frank, Britt, author.
Title: Align your mind: tame your inner critic and make peace with your
shadow using the power of parts work / Britt Frank, LSCSW.
Description: [New York] : Tarcher, [2025] | Includes index.
Identifiers: LCCN 2024041698 (print) | LCCN 2024041699 (ebook) |
ISBN 9780593850770 (hardcover) | ISBN 9780593850794 (epub)
Subjects: LCSH: Psychotherapy. | Personality. |
Self-consciousness (Awareness) | Spiritual life.
Classification: LCC RC480 .F66 2025 (print) |
LCC RC480 (ebook) | DDC 616.89/14—dc23/eng/20241223
LC record available at https://lccn.loc.gov/2024041698
LC ebook record available at https://lccn.loc.gov/2024041699

Printed in the United States of America
1st Printing

Book design by Shannon Nicole Plunkett

The authorized representative in the EU for product safety and
compliance is Penguin Random House Ireland, Morrison Chambers, 32
Nassau Street, Dublin D02 YH68, Ireland, https://eu-contact.penguin.ie.

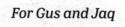

For Gus and Jaq

Contents

Author's Note

*A*lign *Your Mind* is geared toward people who experience an inner monologue. Not everyone experiences their minds the same way, so for those who do not identify with the experience of "hearing their thoughts," this book may not be helpful. None of the tools, techniques, exercises, or information in *Align Your Mind* are intended to replace medical care or mental health treatment.

Always speak with your doctor before going off medication. The content of this book does *not* refer to auditory hallucinations, spiritually sourced voices, or any voices that tell you to hurt yourself or others. If your thoughts are disturbing to you or you feel unsafe or triggered at any point, immediately put this book down. If you are in crisis, call 911 or go to the nearest emergency room. If you are experiencing suicidal thoughts, text 988 to access the suicide crisis lifeline. To contact the National Alliance on Mental Illness helpline, please call 800-950-NAMI (6264), Monday through Friday, 10 a.m. to 10 p.m. ET, or send an email to helpline@nami.org.

Align Your Mind contains ideas from Internal Family Systems therapy, Jungian psychology, philosophy, ecology, and neuroscience. This book does not address issues related to social injustice, gender, or sexuality. Client names and identifying details have been changed. Though efforts were made to ensure the accuracy of all information as of the time of writing this book, science is always subject to change without notice, and intangibles like "the mind" are always subject to interpretation—no one knows with absolute certainty how the mind works or what consciousness is. As Neil deGrasse Tyson put it, "After the laws of physics, everything else is opinion."

Take what's useful from these pages and leave the rest.

Foreword

Over the course of twenty years in executive search, stewarding thousands of people through massive moments of life interruption and career shift, I heard a lot of hairy, scary goals and dreams. Do you want to know how I knew who would achieve success and who would not? Success came always, and only, to the ones who felt so much respect and awe for their outsize ideas of their own potential that they could manage but a whisper that they existed.

One part of them wanted it, and another part of them was cowed by it. It was interesting, and it was confusing. It was exciting, and it was terrifying. Promise, but pressure. Clear, but opaque. And all these wide-ranging parts were about to go to battle inside them, with only one able to win. These are the "parts" that Britt Frank so beautifully describes in *Align Your Mind*. For so many years, I felt confused, mixed up, messed up. How could one part of me want something, see something, be certain I was going to go for it (even if I didn't yet know how), while another part of me was at the very same moment warning me to slow down, step back, and stop?

I spent years working to quiet these voices.

In researching my latest book, I even went so far as to interview more than a hundred glass-ceiling shatterers, Olympic medalists, start-up unicorns, and (this is important!) everyday people like you and me. I was in search of an answer to how they pushed aside doubt and uncertainty and dread and impostor syndrome.

Yes, I spent years working to quiet these voices.

And I spent years failing to quiet these voices.

I came to understand that the very people who thrived in these moments of promise and uncertainty, of pressure and potential, of uncertainty and excitement—a moment I now call Wonderhell—didn't waste time trying to quiet these voices. In fact, they paused to listen to them, learn from them, and grow from them. So you can imagine my delight to learn from Britt that the solution to aligning our mind isn't actually about banishing our inner critic or fighting with ourselves or telling our inner voices to quiet down.

I mean, whew, right?

What if all these voices—these parts—are in there for a reason? What if we aren't supposed to quiet them, but to actually listen to them?

In fact, every single person I ever met who accomplished everything they ever wanted in life did it specifically by hearing those parts not as limitations, but as invitations. They didn't fear that their brains were broken, riddled with anxiety, an inner critic, or a self-saboteur. They knew these parts of themselves were exceptionally helpful allies, each of which played valuable roles and made contributions that would eventually result in even greater success.

So they paused. They listened to them. They learned from them. They grew from them.

They made these parts a part of their story, fully integrated and momentum-building, and not something against which they fruitlessly fought.

All of us are trapped by what we think is possible, and yet what seems possible is based only on where we've been and what has been possible so far. Imagine that you are at the bottom of a mountain and looking at the top. It looks beautiful, that mountaintop, and you are thinking, *I want to go there.*

Good for you! You set a goal! And a hard one at that. But then a funny thing happens.

Halfway up the mountain, you see a sign for a scenic overlook, and you cut through the bush to find yourself looking out at the top of your mountain . . . and the other mountaintops beyond and above that. None of them were visible from the ground. But here, halfway up, with one goal in mind, you suddenly have a new, harder, more exciting goal.

You picked up this book because you are on a personal journey to optimize this one big, juicy life you've got, to expand what you think is possible, and to capture the meaning and purpose that you were put on this earth to embody. You might be reading this book as an accompaniment to therapy; you might be reading it on your own. In either case, as you move through the pages of this book and learn more about how the brain works, mountaintop beyond mountaintop will appear in full view, each inviting you to dare to become everything you've ever imagined (or even not yet imagined) that you could be.

There are multitudes within you.

Each of those multitudes has an opinion.

Either they can fight with each other or you can align your mind so that they work together.

The choice is yours.

—Laura Gassner Otting,
Wall Street Journal **bestselling author of**
Wonderhell: Why Success Doesn't Feel Like
It Should . . . and What to Do About It

Align Your Mind

Introduction

The Surprising Truth About Your Mind

I am large, I contain multitudes.

—**Walt Whitman**

Imagine yourself on your best day. Life is still busy and complicated, but somehow you manage to zip through the obstacle course of work, family, and friends without getting stuck. Your inner critic is unusually quiet and contented. You can see the whole chessboard and confidently select your moves and countermoves. A surge of "hold my beer" energy emboldens you to pick up a pickleball racket (or whatever new thing you want to try), and all the competing voices in your head stop their shouting and should-ing. The gap between what you know you *want* to do and what you *actually* do is closed. Despite life's uncertainty, you can execute decisions without self-doubt, and you feel—for a moment—like the best version of yourself. Life is good.

This state is what positive psychologist Mihaly Csikszentmihalyi coined *flow*. A flow state is when you're fully immersed in what you're doing without tripping over your thoughts. You feel present and energized. Wonder and possibility fill the spaces typically occupied by overwhelm and confusion. External circumstances remain imperfect, but somehow you feel solid and grounded. Flow states show up in emergencies when you stay almost eerily calm during a disaster. They also come online during peak performance. When you watch a world-class dancer float through a routine or an athlete seem to easily defy gravity, you're likely witnessing a flow state.

For those of us who aren't Everest climbers or Cirque du Soleil performers, a flow state might look like pulling off both the school pickup *and* the work conference in the same day. Or hitting the gym at five a.m. even when it's rainy and freezing. Or having a calm conversation with your partner even though part of you wants to pour a bucket of paint on their head. When you're in a flow state, there are no dueling factions in your mind. You glimpse the "real" you. The person you sense you're capable of being. The person who has both clarity about what to do *and* the willingness to act. During flow states, your mind and body align. When you're in alignment, you feel like you're moving with the current of life—not thrashing against it.

Sounds great, right? Except there's one major problem—this blissful state is often quick to vanish.

Suddenly, instead of clearheaded decisiveness, you feel an army of squirrels descend into your mind (and your home), and now you're running for dear life, throwing acorns into the air.* The person who gracefully whizzed through their day and felt reasonably good about themselves disappears, and the super-adult, epic version of you is replaced by someone else. This version of you struggles to move the wet laundry into the dryer, so the clothes sit in the machine until they turn crusty and grow mildew. The couch seems to develop a locking mechanism you can't escape. Scheduling time with friends? Impossible. The body you were at peace with yesterday is flawed and wrong from every angle today. This ver-

---

* Squirrels are scary.

sion of you ignores texts and voice mails as they pile up and then feels too guilty to do anything about it.

So what's going on here? Why is it that one day you can stay calm but on another you're a rampaging Hulk? Why can you nail it during your sales presentation, but still feel an inner heckler pelting you with thoughts of *not-enough-ness*? Why is it that no matter how old you get, as soon as you go home for the holidays you feel like a moody teenager? Is it because you're fake? Or crazy?*

Nope.

The reason you feel like a kaleidoscope of different people on different days (and hear a cacophony of inner voices) is not because you're disordered, nor is it because you're a hypocrite. It's because your mind—and my mind and those of all other humans—is beautifully complex. Many of us were taught it's "just us" up in our heads, but as psychologist Jay Noricks observed, "The normal sense we have of being a unitary I or me is an illusion." More simply put, *your mind is made of different parts*. And when your parts are at odds with one another, it can be difficult to feel like the best version of yourself.

What's the Solution?

The surprising solution offered in *Align Your Mind* is not new and it's not a flash-in-the-pan social media trend—it's been around since humans discovered how to paint words onto papyrus. It's not a fringe, niche-y idea, either—this information crosses a broad spectrum of cultures and disciplines. You'll find it in science, philosophy, psychology, spirituality, and indigenous traditions. When I first learned

---

* There's no such thing as a crazy person. I use the word here to refer to a feeling, not to an actual state. *Crazy* is a personal judgment, not a biological reality.

about it, I was both stunned by its obviosity and thoroughly annoyed that no one had told me about it sooner. This surprising solution is called *parts work*. In the 10,000-plus hours I've sat with clients, I've yet to see a single method, model, or framework be as effective or move people forward as quickly (or as sustainably) as parts work.

What Is Parts Work?

Parts work is a process that allows you to explore, understand, and connect with the different aspects of your mind. It's a different way to think about thinking. *Parts work* is an umbrella term under which a diverse group of approaches* fall, but simply put, it's a set of techniques that allow you to work *with* your mind instead of fighting it. The goal of parts work isn't to get rid of your parts—it's to *lead* them. You don't need to banish your inner critic—parts work helps you train it to become a powerful ally. You don't need to kill your ego—parts work helps you decode its messages.

While many different types of therapy utilize parts work, you don't need to be in crisis, you don't need a decade of psychoanalysis, and you don't need advanced neuroscience training to do it. Even if you think things in your life are fine, there's more for you waiting to be discovered. As author and therapist Ralph De La Rosa put it, "Just as our bodies are made of many parts that form a dynamic, interwoven system that works together, so it is with our psyches. We are more awake, alive, and complex than we know."

What does that mean?

Have you ever felt like you were at war with your mind?

---

* Parts-work-based modalities include Gestalt therapy, voice dialogue, inner child work, psychodrama, psychosynthesis, transactional analysis, Jungian analysis, and ego state therapy. My personal favorite is Internal Family Systems, created by Dr. Richard Schwartz.

Most people would quickly say yes—it's a very human dilemma. But when you battle yourself—*who is battling whom*? Who is doing the arguing and who is doing the listening? Parts work pioneer Dr. Richard Schwartz developed Internal Family Systems (IFS) in response to clients' descriptions of various parts within themselves. I discovered IFS while neck-deep in a sadness swamp of addictions, eating disorders, depression, and anxiety. Learning to approach my mind as a system of parts changed *everything* for me—and it can for you, too. When you realize your mind is made of different parts, the internal arguing starts to make sense. But if you're like me, you learned your personality is set in stone, the brain you have is the brain you're stuck with, and your mind is a single thing.

This isn't a new problem:

- In 1908's *Anne of Green Gables*, the protagonist laments, "There's such a lot of different Annes in me. I sometimes think that is why I'm such a troublesome person. If I was just the one Anne it would be ever so much more comfortable, but then it wouldn't be half so interesting."
- In 1855's *Song of Myself*, Walt Whitman wrote, "Do I contradict myself? Very well then, I contradict myself."
- Two thousand years ago (give or take), the apostle Paul wrote, "I do not understand what I do. For what I want to do I do not do, what I hate I do."

No wonder we all feel bonkers sometimes.

In *Mindsight*, clinical psychiatry professor and author Dr. Daniel Siegel writes (italics mine), "We must accept our multiplicity, the fact that we can show up quite differently in our athletic, intellectual, sexual, spiritual—or many other—states. The key to well-being is *collaboration across states*, not some rigidly homogeneous unity. The notion that we can have a single, totally consistent way of being is both idealistic and unhealthy." But most of us (me included) were never taught that our minds are made of different parts. As Dr. Schwartz put it, "While it may sound creepy or crazy at first to think of yourself as a multiple personality, I hope to convince you that it's actually quite empowering. It's only disturbing because multiplicity has been pathologized in our culture."

Who This Book Is For

This book is for anyone who wants to feel more empowered, to make decisions faster, and to understand themselves better. Most of us have tried (and failed) to logic our way into good decisions, to positive-think ourselves through impostor-y moments, or to ignore our inner critics. Who among us hasn't felt out of alignment? To be *in alignment* means to be in a position of agreement or alliance. When your choices are aligned with your values and beliefs, you feel empowered and centered. When you're aligned, you become the best version of yourself, and you enter a state of flow. When you're doing things that *don't* align with who you want to be, the result is unease and lack of control. Consider these nine questions:

Have you ever:

1. Argued with yourself?

2. Shrunk down due to a critical inner voice?

3. Thought to yourself, *I don't know why I just said that?*

4. Thought to yourself, *I don't know why I just did that?*

5. Struggled with overthinking?

6. Felt disconnected from yourself?

7. Tried to start a healthy new habit but found yourself stuck in the same old patterns?

8. Grappled with what you really wanted?

9. Dealt with impostor syndrome?

If you answered yes to any of the above, this book can help.

Modern psychology is quick to label people as either mentally healthy or mentally ill, "normal" or disordered. As a licensed clinician, I was trained to view the mind through the lens of brokenness. If someone checks enough boxes off a big list (aka the DSM*), they get a diagnosis.† But if this approach were useful, we wouldn't see the growing epidemic of anxious, stressed, burned-out people. To get unstuck, we need a different way to think about thinking. Rather than viewing our behavior, thoughts, and feelings solely through the "what's wrong with me?" filter, I prefer including author Bill Plotkin's take: "There's been too little consideration of what is inherently right and inspiring about human beings."

Your mind is not a problem to be solved, but a mystery to be explored.

A Map of Your Mind

If your mind had a shape, it would look more like a wheel than a single point.

---

* The *Diagnostic and Statistical Manual of Mental Disorders (DSM)* is a highly politicized list of symptoms that do not take trauma or environment into account. That said, it's important because it allows people access to services and accommodations.

† There's no shame in having a mental health diagnosis. And it's important to know that most therapists are not trained to consider trauma or environmental factors before assigning a diagnosis.

Your mind is not this:

It's more like this:

At the center of the wheel is the person in charge, the "I" at the center of the storm. Philosophers call this the Essential Self or the True Self. Spiritual practitioners call it Christ Consciousness, Soul, or Jiva. Some religions call it the Holy Spirit, Neshama, or Atman. In this book we'll use Internal Family Systems language: Self (with a capital S). Personality psychologist Gordon Allport defined Self as "the 'I' experienced by an individual." He also noted, "It is much easier to feel the self than to define the self." By whatever name you call it, when you operate from the center of your "wheel," life rolls along more smoothly.

If Self is the center of the wheel, all the different spokes represent the different parts of your mind. You might have a part of you who loves to watch cooking shows in complete solitude, but another part who loves to get out and explore the city with friends. You may love your newborn baby with all your heart, but part of you misses uninterrupted, pre-parenthood sleep. When you operate from Self, you can manage all the different "spokes," and you access a sense of flow. If you've ever had trouble locating your Self, the techniques in this book will help you find it.

How to Use This Book

If you're familiar with my work, you know being told what to do spikes my blood pressure. (And if you're new here, welcome. Fun fact about me—I don't like being told what to do.) I won't read a book if instructed to "start at the beginning and stop at the end." If you can relate to this, you're my people. If you're a start-to-finish person, you can still read this book the "regular" way, but in the spirit of the Choose Your Own Adventure series, you have three other options:

Option One:
I Have No Time to Shower, Let Alone Read

Life is busy. There are times when we have zero bandwidth and zero time to make a dent in the to-be-read stack. I get it. For this option, you don't have to invest a lot of energy and you don't need to find a quiet place or commit hours of your day. Instead, you can use the **scan, skim, skip** method. Scan through the chapter titles and see which ones seem interesting. Skim through the chapter headings. If you see something that catches your eye, mark the page so you can return to it later. Ignore the footnotes and skip straight to the end of each chapter, where you'll find a bullet point summary. This method works great if you're a read-in-the-bathroom kind of person. If you're not a read-in-the-bathroom kind of person, consider trying it—you'll be in there for at least a few minutes every day, which gives you plenty of time to invoke the scan, skim, skip approach. At the end of each chapter, you'll have the option to do a quick (one to five minutes) exercise.

Option Two:
I'm Curious, but Short on Time

You don't need to read this book in order. Look through the chapter titles and jump straight to the ones that feel relevant to you. If you have a pesky inner critic but great relationships, skip the relationship chapter and check out "Your Inner Critic Is Your Ally." If you're on top of all your responsibilities but struggle to play and enjoy life, jump to "Becoming More You." If you have time to focus on only one chapter, consider "No Motivation Required," as it will give you practical and actionable tools. Ignore the footnotes. At the end of each chapter is a summary of the material—feel free to jump straight to the end of each chapter *before* you read it to make sure the information feels relevant. After the chapter summary, you'll have the option to do a short exercise that will take five to fifteen minutes.

Option Three: Tell Me All the Things

If you want the deep-dive option, grab a pen, a highlighter, and a journal. You don't have to read this book in order, though you may consider starting with chapter 1 before jumping around, since it will give you an overview of the concepts. Skip over the footnotes but return to them later for bread-crumb trails and miscellaneous trivia. Read through all the chapters (in whatever order you want), do the suggested exercises, and as a side quest, check out the suggested reading at the back of the book and pick a few that catch your interest. At the end of each chapter, you'll have the option to do an in-depth exercise that will take fifteen to forty-five minutes.

No matter which option you choose, throughout the next nine chapters we'll take a journey beyond the vortex of to-do lists and daily concerns that occupy your time and energy. Within your complex and mysterious mind, you'll discover more creativity, capacity, and power than you ever dreamed possible.

Disclaimer

The tools and information you'll find here represent the information that I've found most useful in my personal and professional practice thus far. No one really knows with absolute certainty how the mind or the brain works. The architecture of the brain remains as mysterious as Stonehenge or the ancient pyramids. It's unlikely that humans will ever unlock every secret held by the billions of neurons in our heads. Socrates was spot-on when he wrote, "The more I know, the more I realize I know nothing." As with anything, take what's useful from these pages and leave the rest. And as I mentioned in the author's note—but it bears repeating—when I talk about the "voices in your head," I'm referring to your *inner thoughts/inner monologue*; I am *not* referring to auditory hallucinations or voices that tell you to hurt yourself or other people.

You Are Not Broken

Before we start, it's important to note the goal of this work isn't to change yourself—it's to *know* yourself. Many people try to change habits by white-knuckling through rigid and restrictive programs. But when you try to change a behavior without understanding the origin of the behavior, it's easy to get stuck on a loop of "I'll start again tomorrow" or "maybe someday . . ."

When you align your mind, your choices start to make sense. You'll realize *you* make sense. You're not lazy, crazy, or unmotivated—no one is.* And you don't need to stay stuck.

---

* If you read *The Science of Stuck*, you'll recognize this sentiment. *Lazy* is a moral judgment, not a biological reality. *Crazy* is a pejorative used to label things that defy understanding. But there's no such thing as a crazy person. And all humans are motivated—our brains are motivated either to mobilize in a direction of our choice or to survive a real or perceived threat.

You're not lazy, crazy, or unmotivated—no one is.

Once you get the hang of the tools, even long-standing patterns of thinking, being, and doing start to shift—no internal war required. You don't have to fight your brain and you don't have to fear your mind.

Is this process messy and sometimes uncomfortable? Yes. Is it worth the trouble? Without a doubt. As Jungian analyst and celebrated author Dr. Clarissa Pinkola Estés put it, "As with any descent to the unconscious, there comes a time when one simply hopes for the best, pinches one's nose, and jumps into the abyss. If this were not so, we would not have needed to create the words heroine, hero, or courage." If you don't feel quite ready to jump into the abyss, remember this—you don't need readiness, you need only willingness.

Off we go . . .

Part One

What Is Parts Work?

In the first section of this book, you'll be introduced to the basic concepts in parts work. In the next three chapters you'll learn to recognize and communicate with your internal parts, uncover the connection between your mind and body, and mine the hidden gifts of your shadow. This section provides you with foundational information and practical tools to begin your journey.

Chapter 1

Everyone Has Multiple Personalities

Imagine If They Could All Get Along

> *I have lots of inner voices . . . It's busy up there.*
>
> —Robin Ince

Everyone has voices in their heads. You have them and so do I. Your friends have them and so do your coworkers. Voices that criticize you for not doing enough. Voices that blame you for taking on too much. Voices that tell you it's time to stop the nightly cycle of DoorDash and doomscrolling, and voices that nag you to go to the gym when you'd rather watch just *one* more Netflix stand-up special. Sometimes those voices sound like peppy cheerleaders, but more often they resemble playground bullies. On any given day, our heads are filled with conversations, questions, and concerns. Whether you're facing a high-stakes life choice or indecision about dinner, you've probably argued with yourself.

Argued with yourself. Full stop.

Have you ever stopped to consider that sentiment— "argued with yourself"—and what it *really* means? We all say it. We all do it. But who is arguing with whom? Who mischievously whispers, "You've already blown it, so might as well blow it big and we'll start again tomorrow"? And when that happens (which it does to everyone), who feels shame and guilt the next morning?

As a psychotherapist, I get asked this question most often, from billionaire business owners to teenagers, athletes, entrepreneurs—everyone. Same question. You might recognize it:

Why is it that part of me knows exactly what I need to do, but this other part of me seems to take over, and I just can't seem to get it done?

Sound familiar? I can relate to this dilemma, too.

Prior to becoming a licensed psychotherapist and a reasonably functional adult, I worked in the corporate world. On paper, everything looked fine. I had a shiny new degree from Duke University and a shiny new job at an advertising agency. I hit my KPIs (which is a silly acronym for *key performance indicators,* an unnecessary mouthful) and I met all my deadlines. But at night, a very different story was playing out. At night, my life was a chaotic blur of dysfunction and addiction. It's very strange, and not all uncommon, to discover that there are people smoking crystal meth on Tuesdays and then showing up for budget meetings on Wednesdays.

And that was me. That was my hot mess train wreck of a life.

People ask, "How did you let things get that bad?" But keep in mind, *no one* wakes up one morning and says, "I think I'll destroy my life today." But seemingly insignificant choices and compromises and small, nearly imperceptible shifts over time added up to a *very* big problem. Part of me knew I needed help. Part of me was quite aware that the dynamic in my home rivaled anything you'd see on reality television. But this *other* part of me seemed determined to sabotage my efforts to get unstuck. Life limped along until I reached the point of total collapse. I don't like the term *rock bottom*,* but if there was a rock-bottom moment, what happened next would qualify.

It was the night before a big work event. Someone else had bought the drugs. Someone else had brought the pipe. And the part of me who justified my behavior insisted, "It doesn't *really* count as an addiction if there are other people around." (For any non–drug users here, that was my version of the time-honored axiom "Calories don't count if you're eating someone *else's* french fries.")

But then things took a turn.

It was five a.m., and the party was over. And there I was, sitting in a bathroom, with a pipe in my hand—completely alone. I'd love to tell you that a higher power intervened in that moment and convinced me to stop, but that's not what happened. I made a choice, and I took the hit. But as I clicked the lighter and inhaled the plume of foul-smelling smoke, my story took a strange twist. At that moment, all the different parts of myself stopped arguing, stopped justifying, stopped spinning in circles. At that moment, all the parts of myself came together in their little boardroom inside my head, and they said, "We've reached a unanimous decision. You have a problem."

What does this have to do with you?

Not everyone can identify with having a drug addiction or a mental health challenge, but we all have our version of that story. We all have—dare I say—our own "bathroom-floor moments." Moments when we're at odds with ourselves, and moments

Everyone has multiple personalities—imagine if they all got along?

---

* I define *rock bottom* as anywhere you decide you are done with a behavior. It doesn't need to include a huge dramatic problem. But I don't like the term because you can hit rock bottom, take out a shovel and pickax, and keep digging.

when we're stuck in patterns that desperately need to break. These are the moments for which this book is designed. Because if you think about it, it's fair to say *everyone* has multiple personalities—imagine if they all got along?

They can.

The Surprising Truth About Your Mind

The surprising truth is this: Your mind is made of *parts*. There's nothing pathological, mystical, or strange about it. You experience your parts every day. There's the part of you who is committed to an early morning journal practice, but there's also that *other* part of you who pounds an iron fist on the snooze button. There's the part of you who would love to take up a creative hobby like music or painting, but there's also a part who says, *It's too late for that—and besides, you have* way *too much on your plate.* When I talk about the different parts of the mind, people tend to get worried and ask, "Are you saying I have multiple personality disorder?"

No.

I'm not talking about multiple personality disorder. That's a totally separate thing (and an outdated term to boot). What used to be called multiple personality disorder is now called dissociative identity disorder (DID), and DID is a reasonable response to extreme trauma. This book is not about disorders or extreme trauma. And it's not about how to fix your mind or how to change your mind—it's about how to *align* your mind. When your mind is aligned, you feel more connected to yourself and more in control of your choices. Just like misaligned wheels on your car or a misaligned spine will cause problems, the same is true for your mind. You can have all the information in the world, but insight without alignment equals stuckness. Forget about waiting for the stars to align—when your *mind* is aligned, life works better.

Out of Alignment

The idea of alignment can feel esoteric and abstract, so let's define it in more concrete terms: To be in alignment means your thoughts and actions match your values and beliefs. Not what you think *should* be your values or what your partner/family/society thinks *should* be your beliefs, but what is genuinely true for *you*. Let's examine a few real-life stories that illustrate what being out of alignment looks like:

> *Cruz, thirty-two, came into therapy puzzled by his unhappiness. He worked as a high-paid programmer at a tech start-up, his two boys were healthy and active at school and in soccer, and his relationship with his partner was—for the most part—smooth sailing. But Cruz constantly battled feelings of heaviness, lethargy, and joylessness. An inner voice kept nagging at him to blow everything up and run away. And another voice would immediately shame him for feeling anything but grateful. To escape this inner conflict, Cruz came home every evening and numbed out for hours on his phone. In his words, "My life is fine. Things at home are fine. But it's like there's no sound—everything feels like it's on mute. What's wrong with me?"*

Cruz had a part of his mind who thought he should always be grateful. But another part resented his work as a programmer—what he *really* wanted (and what he had always wanted) was to be a painter. Learning to listen to—and align with—these parts of his mind gave Cruz clarity to make different decisions. While ultimately he decided to keep his current job, taking classes at a local art school allowed him to feel more fully aligned and to permit sound and color to come back into his life. Creating alignment wasn't just a personal win for Cruz; it also marked the beginning of a healing journey for his whole family.

Similarly, Jody's story below highlights the challenges that arise when external actions are out of alignment with internal truth.

> *Jody, forty-one, suffered from classic "good girl" conditioning. She volunteered for the PTA, was always the first person at her church offering to drive someone to an appointment or to bring a meal, and her answer for every request—from everyone—was yes. There was a part of Jody who resented her life and wanted time to focus on herself, but whenever she tried to set boundaries, another part of her felt so bloated with guilt she'd abandon her self-care plans and return to being the yes-person. When Jody started suffering from frequent migraines with no medical explanation, she found herself in my office.*

Jody genuinely loved helping other people, but there was a part of her who *really* needed to step away from always being the helper so she could focus on other things. Ignoring this part of herself created a resentment loop where Jody became so exhausted and misaligned, her body produced physical symptoms.* When she learned to connect with the parts of herself who needed alone time (while also learning to keep the guilty parts satisfied), her energy and vitality returned, and she learned to cultivate a sustainable mix of generosity and self-care.

Jody's difficulty with boundaries is similar to Carrie's predicament. Carrie's parts who desired an intimate relation-

---

* Always go to a medical doctor to rule out medical causes of a symptom before trying a psychological intervention.

ship clashed repeatedly with those who chased the high of unavailable partners.

> *Carrie, twenty-four, sought therapy to help with her self-reported intimacy issues. More than anything, she wanted to be in a healthy relationship and to have children. Exasperated, she told me, "I've tried everything to break this pattern, but nothing ever works." Year after year, Carrie glued glossy magazine images onto vision boards, scrawled affirmations on her mirror, and regularly indulged in the clichéd self-care standard—candlelit bubble baths. Nevertheless, she repeatedly chose partners who were emotionally unavailable and narcissistic. Part of her knew a relationship with a person whom she saw only between the hours of eleven p.m. and four a.m. was not going to fare well. But another part compelled her to continue the same toxic relationship patterns. Even though logically she knew it was a bad idea to answer the late-night "hey . . . you up?" texts, inevitably Carrie ended up on a shame-filled predawn drive home. Wash, rinse, repeat.*

Though Carrie wanted to be in a functional relationship, part of her inner world was so accustomed to the drama of bad relationships that she continued to seek partners who met the criteria of emotionally unavailable and narcissistic. Rather than getting rid of this part, Carrie learned to work with her parts, especially the ones who felt comfort with the familiarity of unavailable people. A few years after we completed therapy, she sent me a photo from her beautiful beach wedding to an emotionally available partner whom she adored.

What do Cruz, Jody, and Carrie have in common? Their behaviors and patterns directly opposed their values and beliefs. They were all living *out* of alignment. Even though parts of them wanted to be creative, to value self-care, and to be in equitable relationships, powerful pulls from *other* parts called the shots. In each story, no one needed to abandon or silence their parts. Instead, they discovered the transformative power of *alignment* with their parts.

Benefits of Parts Work

Why should you bother learning how to do parts work? Because ultimately, as Dr. Daniel Siegel put it in *Mindsight,* "If you have a fight with yourself, who can win?" Though parts work can feel cumbersome at first, eventually it becomes second nature, much like learning a second language. When you become fluent in another language, you expand your outer world. When you learn to speak the language of parts, you'll expand both your outer *and* your inner worlds. Benefits of parts work includes:

- Insight into who you *really* are
- Clarity on what you *really* want
- Energy to move toward your dreams
- Wisdom about your relationships
- Courage to do big things

What I didn't know then, and what you're holding in your hands now, is the information that helped me simplify (and demystify) parts work so I could align my mind—and how you can, too.

A Warning About Parts Work

Admittedly, parts work feels odd and uncomfortable when you start. Why? Most of us learned to think of our minds as a singular thing. *Mind multiplicity*—the idea that your mind is made of parts—is a dramatic departure from our normal way of thinking. But normal does not equal optimal. In *Parts Psychology,* psychologist and anthropologist Dr. Jay Noricks writes, "The idea that we all have multiple personalities—but not a disorder of personalities—may at first be shocking. But the evidence for this normal multiplicity . . . is so powerful that even the most skeptical of readers may change their minds."

The idea you're *not* alone in your head—that you're constantly accompanied by a colorful cast of characters with competing roles and agendas—can initially feel jarring and borderline offensive. When it comes to changing our minds, humans don't have the greatest track record:

- When Galileo suggested the sun, not the Earth, was the center of the galaxy,* he was arrested by the Inquisition.
- Louis Pasteur was ridiculed for suggesting that infections were spread by invisible germs.
- When conspiracy theorist Charlie Veitch changed his mind and declared the American government did *not* cause and then cover up the events of 9/11, he was threatened and then canceled by his community.

Facepalm.

Fortunately, as my friend David McRaney, journalist and author of *How Minds Change,* put it, "We each have the power to give up old beliefs, to replace old ignorance with new wisdom, to shift our attitudes in light of new evidence . . . the ability to realize we are wrong is baked right into the gooey mess of neurons wobbling around in every human head." It's good to be wrong about beliefs like "This is just who I am,"

---

* Technically, Copernicus was the originator of the "sun is the center" model of the universe during the Renaissance. He did not face persecution. When Galileo affirmed the Copernican heliocentric model, he was labeled a heretic and put under house arrest.

"I'm such a procrastinator," "I can't relax," or "I can't do big things." Imagine if you could create a collaborative relationship with your mind—and even enjoy spending time with it?

You can.

I fell down the rabbit hole because I was willing to do *anything* to escape the voices in my head. But the most potent psychological medicine for anxiety, insecurity, self-doubt, and impostor syndrome doesn't live outside your mind—it patiently waits for you down the less traveled road *inside*. This book will help you to navigate this road and avoid the pitfalls and "oops" lessons I had to learn the hard way. The working assumptions of *Align Your Mind* are:

Your brain is on your side. Your brain isn't wired for happiness. It's wired for survival. Sometimes the things we think of as anxiety attacks or unwanted thoughts are our brain's best efforts to help us.

Your brain and your mind are not the same. The brain is a physical organ. A neurosurgeon could reach inside your head and touch your brain. The mind is not physical. Since Aristotle, people continue to debate the definition of *mind*. In this book, when we talk about the parts of your *brain,* that includes tangibles like your amygdala, frontal cortex, and nervous system. When we talk about the parts of your *mind,* that refers to intangibles like your inner critic or inner child.

Your mind is not one thing, but a system of parts. A tree is a single organism, but it is made of parts—bark, branches, leaves, and roots. A car is one object, but it is also made of parts—tires and wires and steel and glass. If you look at even the smallest things under a microscope, you'll discover grains of sand, snowflakes, and even atoms can be broken down into smaller parts. Every complex system is made of parts—including your mind.

You can communicate with your parts. You talk to yourself every day. You hear yourself think thoughts every day. Parts work isn't a dramatic departure from what you're already doing—it's a different way of doing it. Think of parts work as couples therapy between you and your mind.

There are no bad parts. While clearly there are bad *behaviors,* all parts have value and there are no bad parts.* As Internal Family Systems creator Dr. Richard Schwartz put it in *No Bad Parts,* "When parts do take over, we don't shame them. Instead, we get curious and use the part's impulse as a trailhead to find what is driving it that needs to be healed." While an explanation is not a synonym for an excuse, it's useful to separate your *parts* from their *behaviors.*

Your parts have different personalities. The word *personality* is often thought of as a single thing with only one per customer, and what you got is all you get. But your parts all have different personalities. Think of your parts like a cast of characters—each character has a unique set of likes, dislikes, inclinations, and traits. If you haven't seen Pixar's *Inside Out* movies, they are a fun exploration of this concept. Riley, the protagonist in the movie, needed *all* her parts and *all* their personalities—even the ones who felt sad, disgusted, anxious, and hotheaded.

If you're more of a visual learner and glazed over that last part, here's an at-a-glance chart:

TERM	DEFINITION
Brain	The three-pound lump of salt, fat, and gray matter between your ears. It's a physical organ. Some describe the brain like a computer's hardware.
Mind	The nonphysical, intangible, conscious thinking function produced by the brain. If the brain is like a computer's hardware, the mind could be described as the software.

---

* "My parts made me do it" is never a valid excuse for causing harm.

TERM	DEFINITION
Parts	If you could put your mind under a microscope, you'd discover that just like your body and your brain are made of parts, your mind is also made of parts. As Dr. Richard Schwartz put it, "Your inner world is real. Parts are not imaginary products or symbols of your psyche; nor are they simply metaphors of deeper meaning . . . what happens in those inner realms makes a big difference in how you feel and live your life."
Personality	You have multiple body parts and multiple personalities. This isn't disordered or abnormal—it's the structure of the human psyche. Each of the different parts of your mind has a different collection of traits, likes, dislikes, fears, concerns, and patterns.

The Problem with Personality

Defining *personality* is problematic. Since you can't touch or see it, there's no way to measure it. Science can be quick to relegate unmeasurable things to the pseudoscience trash heap, but you don't need to put your thoughts in a test tube to know you think them. You don't have to empirically study love to know when you feel it. Even though the term *personality* is subjective and there's no consensus on what it "really" means, you don't need a neuroscience degree to know it when you see it.

What Is Personality?

The word *personality* comes from the Latin word *persona*—a theatrical mask worn by performers to hide their identities.

Just like a show has multiple characters, your mind also has multiple characters, who all play different roles and wear different masks. Some people explain personality in terms of introversion and extroversion. Others think of personality as a person's cornucopia of quirks. If I asked you to tell me about *your* personality, you might share your disdain for group projects, love of stale Peeps, or preference for pets over people. To help organize this mess of definitions and considerations, let's take a minute to sort fact from fiction when it comes to personality:*

Fiction: Your personality is fixed.

Fact: Your personality can change.

Some people believe personality is set in stone and cannot be changed, but neuroscience indicates otherwise. *Neuroplasticity,* in which your brain continues to grow and to create new pathways, is a well-documented phenomenon. If your brain can change its shape, it's reasonable to infer your personality can, too. A University of California article says, "It has long been believed that people can't change their personalities, which are largely stable and inherited. But a review of recent research in personality science points to the possibility that personality traits can change through persistent intervention and major life events."†

Your brain continues to grow and to create new pathways.

Fiction: Personality is genetic.

Fact: Genetics influence but do not determine personality.

---

* The facts presented here are based on the best available information as of the time of writing this book.

† Karen Nikos-Rose, "Can You Change Your Personality?" University of California, January 9, 2020, https://www.universityofcalifornia.edu/news/can-you-change-your-personality.

Genes play a role in personality traits and behavioral tendencies, but they *don't* possess the power to seal your future. Environment, experiences, safety, and access to choices all contribute to personality development. Certain challenges may include a genetic component, but genetics don't always doom you to an inevitable fate. I have a genetic predisposition to severe and persistent mental illness (SPMI) and chronic heart disease, but I do not currently experience symptoms of either. Genetic history serves as a reminder to take precautions in certain areas, but genes are one data point to consider—not an ironclad prophecy.

Fiction: Personality tests are an accurate measure of personality.

Fact: Personality tests are deeply flawed.

In the disturbing but compelling movie *The Silence of the Lambs*, serial killer Hannibal Lecter responds to a personality test with the snarky (and accurate) objection: "You think you can dissect me with this blunt little tool?" There are more than two thousand personality tests available in the U.S. market alone. You might identify as an ISFJ on the Myers-Briggs* indicator, as a five on the Enneagram, or as an S personality on the DiSC assessment. (If you haven't heard of these, a quick Google search of "personality test" results in more than a billion results.) While some tests have potential to be useful on an individual level, *all* personality tests oversimplify human complexity and often fail to consider cultural norms, mood, environment—or the tendency for people to present themselves in a favorable light. While many corporations, organizations, and social media influencers preach the gospel of personality assessments,

---

* Interestingly, Katharine Cook Briggs and her daughter Isabel Briggs Myers, the constructors of the Myers-Briggs Type Indicator, were a mother-daughter duo with no formal training in psychology. Nevertheless, the Myers-Briggs indicator remains one of the most enduring personality tests on the market.

bestselling author and Wharton professor of organizational psychology Adam Grant put it best: "Acceptance by non-experts isn't a marker of validity. It's a signal of popularity."*

Fiction: You have one personality.

Fact: You have multiple personalities.

Your mind is a complex system made of different parts, and each part plays a different role and embodies different personality traits. You may display boldness with some people but feel quiet and reserved around others. Part of you genuinely loves a decluttered home, but another part of you can't bear to throw anything away. You may feel attractive on one day but won't even look at yourself in a mirror on another. If you've ever felt torn between two choices, that's because you have two different parts with two different personalities, each of whom clamors for your time, energy, and resources.

Fiction: Your personality is either normal or disordered.

Fact: There is no such thing as a disordered personality.

This one is controversial—but stay with me. What's considered normal for one person (or one culture) might be considered strange in another. What's normal for me as a highly sensitive person (HSP) can appear odd to people who aren't as emotionally porous.† The binary of *normal* and *disordered* is reductive. When I talk about the fallacy of personality disorders, I often get angry pushback:

---

* Adam Grant wrote a hilarious commentary on the Myers-Briggs in an article on *Medium*. Read it here: https://medium.com/@AdamMGrant /mbti-if-you-want-me-back-you-need-to-change-too-c7f1a7b6970.

† Shout-out to Robert Falconer for his work with Internal Family Systems (IFS) and his examination of the porosity of mind.

What do you mean, there's no such thing as a disordered personality? What about things like narcissism or borderline personality disorder? My life was destroyed by a narcissistic parent. My world turned upside down when I married someone with borderline personality disorder symptoms. Personality disorders are real, and if you disagree, then you're ableist and you're minimizing and invalidating people's pain.

My response? The *symptoms* of personality disorders* are real. The behaviors associated with personality disorders create devastation for both the afflicted and for the people around them.† I personally wrestled with what the mental health world calls borderline personality disorder for more than twenty years and survived a series of narcissistically abusive relationships. I've lived this dilemma from both sides of the relationship (and both sides of the therapy couch). The pain is real. The internal storm and external chaos are undeniable. But here's the caveat—personality disorders are *not* a problem with someone's personality. Personality disorders would more accurately be described as process addictions.

Wait, what? You're saying that personality disorders aren't a personality problem, but that they're process addictions? What's a process addiction?

Unlike a chemical addiction (any addiction where someone ingests a substance), a *process addiction* is when someone repeats a pattern of thinking or acting with increasing severity over time despite negative consequences. A closer examination of personality disorders reveals a startling resemblance

---

* The term *personality disorder* originated in the 1950s. Time for an upgrade.

† Regardless of the origin of these behaviors or what you call them, it is never acceptable to cause harm and it is always acceptable to set boundaries with people. "My personality disorder made me do it" may be an explanation, but it is not an excuse, nor does it ever mean you have to stay in relationship with someone.

to process addictions. When someone has the safety, re-sources, and willingness to address root causes (and when their behaviors are no longer enabled by well-meaning loved ones), symptoms can significantly lessen—and sometimes disappear completely.* Here's another factor to consider in this debate: since personality is *not* singular, it's impossible to categorize it as normal or disordered.

Fiction: Personality development ends at age five.

Fact: Personality development continues through adulthood.

Some people believe personality development stops after age five—which means once you hit kindergarten, you're done. But as human rights activist Malcolm X put it, "Why am I as I am? To understand that of any person, his whole life from birth must be reviewed. All our experiences fuse into our personality. Everything that ever happened to us is an ingredient." Your personality traits crystallize during child-hood but can continue to change and develop throughout adulthood. Every aspect of your life—your education, rela-tionships, bad experiences, corrective experiences, and will-ingness to try new things—has a potential impact on your personality. Novelist Truman Capote once observed, "The average personality reshapes frequently, every few years even our bodies undergo a complete overhaul—desirable or not, it is a natural thing that we should change."

Fiction: Personality is easy to define.

Fact: No universal agreement exists on the definition of personality.

---

* Sometimes it is not internal disease, but a lack of access to quality care and safety that create chronic conditions. And sometimes conditions persist even with adequate care and safety not because a person lacks capacity, but because they lack *willingness*. Can people change? Often the answer is yes. Will they? Often the answer is no.

If you ask a group of psychologists, scientists, and philosophers to define personality, you'll receive a smattering of answers. While we can all agree on what personality looks like in action, no one agrees on what it *is*. In this book, the word *personality* refers to your parts' collection of traits, likes, dislikes, fears, concerns, and patterns. Each of your parts has its own personality. Internal Family Systems creator Dr. Richard Schwartz wrote:

> A part is not just a temporary emotional state or habitual thought pattern. Instead, it is a discrete and autonomous mental system that has an idiosyncratic range of emotion, style of expression, set of abilities, desires, and view of the world. In other words, it is as if we each contain a society of people, each of whom is at a different age and has different interests, talents, and temperaments.

Throughout *Align Your Mind* you'll encounter different parts of your inner world. Just like each of your physical body parts requires a different type of care, each part of your mind requires a different set of tools. You wouldn't give someone cough syrup to stabilize a ruptured spleen, and it's equally unhelpful to use the same intervention on all your parts.

Types of Parts

You have parts whose job is to protect you from harm and parts who spring into action when bad things happen. Some people have parts who adhere to social norms. These parts can show up when you want to impress your boss at an event and hear an inner voice warn, "Maybe *don't* tell the spring break story." With that said, not every person has the same set of parts. Many people who experience neurodivergence do not have parts that help decode social cues. But regardless of which parts show up for you in different situations, *everyone* has parts who like to do odd stuff when no one's around.

TYPE OF PART*	THEIR JOB	CORE NEED	EXAMPLES
Protectors	To prevent pain by any means necessary (even if that means causing different pain)	To maintain safety	Critical parts, saboteurs, controlling parts, perfectionist parts, anxious parts, distracter parts, people-pleaser parts, parts who choose unavailable partners or friends, stressed parts, depressed parts, avoidant parts, stuck parts
Reactors	To soothe you if something bad happens	To stop pain	Drinker/shopper/binger/scroller/numb-out parts, workaholic parts, "stay as busy as possible" parts, dissociated parts, road-rage parts

* This is a general overview and is not an exact science. Sometimes a part can function as a protector *and* a reactor. Sometimes reactive behaviors look the same as protective behaviors. Use this information as a guide, not as gospel.

TYPE OF PART	THEIR JOB	CORE NEED	EXAMPLES
Story Keepers	To carry any pain from your past so you don't have to feel it in the present**	To be witnessed and cared for	Inner child parts, angry teenager parts, tantruming toddler parts, "well-behaved/cause no trouble" parts, rebellious parts
The ones who are wonderfully weird	To help you decompress when you're alone	To express themselves freely without fear of shame or judgment	Nose pickers, toenail peelers, peanut-butter-on-your-finger scoopers, mirror dancers, hairbrush singers, Nerf sword dragon slayers.***

** The Internal Family Systems Model of therapy calls these parts Exiles. In IFS, the core need of an Exile is to be unburdened.

***This column refers to things people *like to do* when they're alone. It does *not* refer to problematic or unwanted behaviors related to obsessive-compulsive disorder.

You Are Not Your Parts

As you read in the intro (if you skipped it, I invite you to go back and skim it), your mind is like a wheel, and at the center of the wheel is your Self with a capital S—the leader of your inner world. Self is like an orchestra conductor, team captain, company CEO, or movie director. When Self is running the show, you can skillfully manage the competing demands from your parts with a sense of ease and flow. How can you tell the difference between your Self and your parts? The Internal Family Systems (IFS) model identifies eight qualities of Self:

The Eight Cs of the Self

1. Compassion
2. Curiosity
3. Clarity
4. Creativity
5. Calmness
6. Confidence
7. Courage
8. Connectedness

If you're not feeling at least one of those eight qualities, it's safe to assume Self is no longer in charge and a part has taken over.* When a part takes over, you no longer feel alignment or flow. This is when you're most likely to feel overreactive, indecisive, or stuck. The solution? Despite the ubiquitous advice to banish or get rid of your parts, the solution isn't to eliminate your parts—it's to *lead* them. IFS calls this *Self-leadership*—the state of being *with* your parts instead of being driven *by* them. The absence of Self-leadership creates the presence of misalignment. Think of a family dinner where you came a bit unglued, a work meeting where you lost your cool, or anytime you caved to the innocent inner voice who claimed, "It'll just be a *quick* Target run." If you want to feel more control over your impulses, more clarity about your decisions, and more confidence with your actions, you'll need to practice Self-leadership. Stay tuned to learn how.

Bottom-Line Takeaways

1. Your mind is not a single thing—it is made of parts.
2. Your parts can talk to you, and you can talk to your parts.
3. Your parts play different roles and can have competing agendas.

---

* The IFS model uses the term *blended* to describe this phenomenon, and *unblended* to describe the process of parts stepping back so Self can take the lead.

4. There's nothing pathological or mysterious about having multiple personalities.

5. When you align with your parts, you feel more like yourself.

6. Parts work is not a new trend—it's been around for thousands of years.

7. The goal of parts work isn't to get rid of or to silence your parts—it's to lead them.

8. There is no such thing as a disordered personality.

9. Behaviors can be good or bad, but there aren't any bad parts.

10. Parts work feels odd and uncomfortable when you first start doing it.

Action Step Options

I have no time (1–5 minutes):
NOTICE YOUR PARTS.

Set a timer for one minute and observe your thoughts. Don't try to change what's happening—simply notice. After the minute is up, check to see if your thoughts sounded like Self (revisit the eight qualities of Self if needed) or if they sounded more like a part. Remind yourself that your parts are not you and that you are not your parts.

I have some time (5–15 minutes):
CONNECT WITH YOUR PARTS.

Do the previous exercise. If your thoughts sounded like a part, ask the part the following questions. (If your thoughts sounded like Self, imagine that you're having a conversation with a worried part.) You can do this exercise in your head or write the answers you hear in your notebook or journal.

1. What are you most worried about right now?
2. What would you like me to know about you?
3. What's one thing I can do right now to help you?

I'll make time (15–45 minutes): INVENTORY YOUR PARTS.

Do both previous exercises. Then fill in the chart below (or copy it into your journal or notebook). You can use the chart in the section on types of parts on page 33 for help. Do your best *not* to judge or shame yourself for your answers. The goal of this exercise is to stimulate curiosity and awareness.

TYPE OF PART	THEIR JOB	CORE NEED	MY PERSONAL EXAMPLES
Protectors	To prevent pain by any means necessary (even if that means causing different pain)	To maintain safety	
Reactors	To soothe you if something bad happens	To stop pain	

TYPE OF PART	THEIR JOB	CORE NEED	MY PERSONAL EXAMPLES
Hidden	To stay out of sight and out of mind	To be listened to and cared for	
The ones who come out when you're alone	To let you be as wild as you need to be	To express freely	

Chapter 2

More Than Mindset

The Brain-Body Connection

"Rabbit's clever," said Pooh thoughtfully.

"Yes," said Piglet, "Rabbit's clever."

"And he has Brain."

"Yes," said Piglet, "Rabbit has Brain."

There was a long silence.

"I suppose," said Pooh, "that that's why he never understands anything."

—A. A. Milne, *Winnie-the-Pooh*

Brains are weird.* Between your ears, you possess a cosmic neuronal universe with the power to conjure joy, love, awe, and inspiration. But your brain is also a cauldron of chemicals that make you feel depressed, stressed, obsessed, and impulsive. Brains compel us to smile at babies, but they also convince us to lie, gossip, and eat en-

---

* Comedian Pete Holmes said it best: "Sing 'Happy Birthday' in your head; we'll all do it. How are you hearing that? It's so normal. We're just like, 'Yeah, I could hear it. No one else could hear it. I could hear it.' There's just a part of you listening, like, 'Yeah, "Happy Birthday."'" What's going on?"

tire sleeves of frozen Thin Mints.* Your brain is an artist, an architect, an evil genius, a benevolent saint, and a botanical garden teeming with complexity and diversity.

Brains work tirelessly to keep us alive, but they also seem to contain a mechanism of self-destruction. The same organ that sets the goals also wrecks them. Have you ever sat down to write an important email, but suddenly you experience an insatiable urge to clean your junk drawer, followed by a six-hour research marathon on Amazon for the perfect organizer? Or maybe you've decided *today* is the day you'll get back to your yoga practice. You roll out your mat, douse your chakras in lavender and eucalyptus oil, and are just about to fill the world with love and light, but then you see your partner's dirty dishes on the table. Instantly, your Zen state morphs into unbridled rage.

It's Called "Going Nuclear" for a Reason

What causes these dizzying personality flips? In chapter 1, we talked about your parts—the cast of characters inside your mind. When your capital-S Self occupies the director's chair, your inner life runs smoothly, and everyone gets along. But sometimes the distinction between Self and parts is blurry, and rather than leading your parts, you get flooded by their emotions and impulses. Instead of feeling mindful, you're now stuck in a state I call *mindfused*.† *Mind fusion* is the psychological equivalent of nuclear fusion.

---

* The serving size for packages of Oreos, Fig Newtons, and Thin Mints is theoretically two cookies, but everyone knows it's really a sleeve.

† *Identity fusion* is a documented phenomenon in social psychology where a person experiences a sense of oneness with a group (often at great personal cost). Mind fusion is the internal equivalent. The Internal Family Systems model calls this being blended with your parts.

During nuclear fusion, two atoms combine (fuse), causing a state of instability followed by a burst of energy. Here's a highly technical, scientifically comprehensive visual of this concept:*

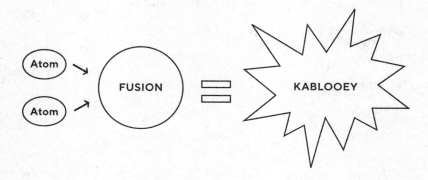

When you experience mind fusion, your "kablooey" can take the form of an explosion (yelling, overreacting, behaving impulsively) or an implosion (procrastinating, feeling stuck or spaced out, overthinking everything, excessive worrying). But when parts step back and allow Self to lead, you're in a *defused* state of mind. You can observe and be *with* your parts instead of feeling overwhelmed by them, and you're able to identify and execute the best decisions available to you in any given moment. Defusing is the key to alignment and flow. Life doesn't always get easier when you defuse, but you *will* feel immediate relief when you do it. The number one goal of parts work is to shift from mindfused to *mindful*.

Defusing is the key to alignment and flow.

---

* I had an entertaining conversation with my husband, a former navy nuclear engineer, about my oversimplification of physics for the purposes of this book.

MINDFUSED versus MINDFUL

MINDFUSED (PARTS-DRIVEN)	MINDFUL (SELF-DRIVEN)
Reactive	Responsive
Overwhelmed	Clearheaded
Myopic	Observant
Scattered	Centered
Preoccupied	Present
Distracted	Focused

Learning to defuse may seem like yet another thing to add to what's already a mountainous to-do list, so it's helpful to remember that *not* doing this work takes more effort than doing it. When you shift from mindfused to mindful, you can think clearly, act quickly, and make better decisions. The benefits of doing this work far outweigh the discomfort of learning it. But before we can talk about the defusing process, including how to do it, we'll need to first dismantle a few mindfulness myths and then take a closer look at the parts of your brain.

Six Mindfulness Myths

Mindfulness dates back thousands of years, but on its journey from ancient philosophers to social media influencers, a haze of misinformation obscured its original purpose. Here are my top six mindfulness myths:

Myth 1:
Mindfulness requires you to clear your mind.
Mindfulness doesn't require you to take a magic eraser to your mind. Your thoughts are not bloodstains at a crime

scene—you don't need to analyze all of them or clean them up. It's a very human experience to occasionally have distorted, unreasonable, and strange thoughts dart across our minds. Mindfulness doesn't mean you have to get rid of your thoughts. Instead, it is the practice of *observing* your thoughts without fusing with them.

Myth 2:
Mindfulness requires meditation.

You can practice mindfulness in the lotus position with your eyes closed and your hands in prayer position, but that's not the only way. The twelve-step recovery world describes mindfulness as "keeping your head where your feet are." Anything you do during your waking hours—including walking, cooking, and driving—can be done mindfully. Mindfulness is about *presence,* not about sticking to a specific *practice*. Do whatever makes sense for you.

Myth 3:
Mindfulness is the cure-all.

Life is complicated, and some problems are best solved by intervention rather than observation. You can't "deep breathe" someone out of an oppressive system or "gratitude journal" your way through a natural disaster. When a tornado strikes, you don't observe the funnel and ponder the wonders of nature*—you get to safety.

Myth 4:
Mindfulness requires dedicated time.

It's great to set aside time for mindfulness if you have it to spare. But it's just as effective to work mindfulness moments *into* your day, rather than forcing yourself to carve hours of time *out* of your day. You can practice mindfulness at an all-

---

* Unless you're Helen Hunt and Bill Paxton circa 1996. IYKYK.

day silent retreat, but you can just as easily practice it during a workout or in the shower.

Myth 5:
Mindfulness equals happiness.

Mindfulness is about awareness, not happiness. You can be mindful and stressed, angry, afraid, or sad. Mindfulness is being with your parts in whatever state they happen to be in; it is *not* about making sure all your parts feel happy.

Myth 6:
Mindfulness is all about mindset.

The word *mindfulness* is a misnomer, because mindfulness is not all in your mind. It is a mental state, but it's also a *physical state*.

How is mindfulness a physical state?

You can be mindful only when your *body* feels safe enough to absorb and process what's happening around you. If your body is in a state of reactivity or distress, mindfulness goes immediately out the window.

More Than Mindset

Imagine you're sitting in a restaurant with a group of friends. You're present, fully engaged with the conversation, and mindful of the surrounding smells, sights, and sounds. Suddenly a rogue lion wanders in through the front door. It pads down the aisles, sniffs the tables, stops right in front of you, and stares you down with huge amber eyes. The air is thick with tension and your body turns to stone; as the lion shakes its mane and growls at you, time stops. Your heart races and beads of sweat drip down your face. Even if you tried to call for help, no sound would come out of your mouth. Fortunately for you, a patron at the next table never leaves home without a stack of tranquilizer darts.

After an apologetic zookeeper retrieved the sleeping lion (and your server comped the meal), you would be understandably shaken up. You wouldn't feel guilty for overreacting. You wouldn't beat yourself up for freezing. There's not a psychotherapist on the planet who'd hear that story, assess your symptoms, and then diagnose you with a case of Acute Lion Reactivity Disorder. In this example, it's clear the problem isn't *inside* you—the problem is *outside* you.

> The problem isn't *inside* you—the problem is *outside* you.

The lion-at-lunch example is silly and extreme, but it's a good way to conceptualize your brain's design. Sometimes what the Western mental health world calls disorders or diseases are the result of brains doing what brains are supposed to do—keep us alive. Even though you're unlikely to bump into an apex predator during your next trip to HomeGoods, your brain doesn't always differentiate between *emotional stressors* and *physical threats*. This is especially relevant when it comes to anxiety.

What Is Anxiety?

Most simply put, anxiety is a series of uncomfortable body sensations. An ominous "come to my office" email or "we need to talk" text can create the same body sensations as a wild animal. Despite technology's sprint toward the future, human brains remain the same. Someday we'll get lattes from robot baristas and therapy sessions from AI holograms, but unlike your phone or computer, your internal software does not update regularly*—it still runs on Brain OS Lion.

---

* Thank you to author and coach Michelle Masters for the phone metaphor.

When your brain perceives a problem but can't identify the source, you'll experience anxiety sensations such as a racing heart, sweaty palms, or a clenched jaw. Because anxiety has no identifiable origin, it can feel like it comes out of nowhere. But anxiety never comes from nowhere; it's not a floating monster waiting to pounce. Most of us (me included) learned inaccurate information about anxiety:

- Anxiety is your ally, not your enemy.
- Anxiety is not a sign that there is something wrong with you.
- Anxiety is a body response, not a mental illness.*
- Anxiety is the check-engine light of your brain's dashboard—it is there to alert you to a problem.

Despite technology's sprint toward the future, human brains remain the same.

But why does my brain think there's a problem when I'm obviously safe and had a great childhood and there isn't anything wrong?

When your brain's check-engine light turns on, the regions of your brain responsible for thinking, logic, and mindfulness turn off.† This is why it can feel impossible to talk your way out of anxiety, to "just stop" when you're feeling panic, or to interrupt racing thoughts with logic. Your brain is programmed to scan for potential threats and opportunities, and it ingests countless pieces of data, much of which is unconsciously processed. In other words, your brain has access to more information than you do. In the lion example, it's easy to see the threat. But in our fast-paced world,

---

* "Anxiety is not a disease" does *not* mean that meds aren't useful in some cases for some people. Never go off your medication without talking to your doctor.

† The idea of turning on and off is a metaphor, not a literal description of neurology.

we walk around all day, every day with lions at our backs. Modern-day lions include:

- Financial insecurity
- Job uncertainty
- Fear of pandemic
- Screen-time overload
- Unaddressed childhood wounds
- Cauliflower pizza

When it comes to life's lions, we often use the words *anxiety* and *fear* interchangeably. But fear and anxiety are not the same, and using accurate language matters if we want to feel better.

In *Your Brain at Work*, author and psychologist Dr. David Rock put it this way: "When you experience significant internal tension and anxiety, you can reduce stress by up to 50% by simply noticing and naming your state." Or as Dr. Daniel Siegel put it, "Name it to tame it." Receiving an unexpected medical bill, watching the news, or being left on "read" causes fear—not anxiety.

Anxiety, Fear, and Worry: What's the Difference?

Anxiety: Uncomfortable body sensations with no identifiable source. Can range from low-grade discomfort to life-threatening.

Fear: Uncomfortable body sensations with a clear origin point.

Worry: Uncomfortable body sensations with a clear origin point—but at a lower intensity than fear.

Why differentiate? Does it really matter if we call things fear, worry, or anxiety?

Yes.

If it's anxiety, it can be hard to pinpoint effective interventions. If it's fear or worry, you can access a wider menu of options. For example, let's take Nathan, a client who came buzzing into my office after a tough day at work, clearly distressed.

Nathan: *Hi. I'm having an anxiety attack.*

Me: *Hi. You've had a day.*

Nathan: *I feel like I'm about to explode and I can barely breathe.*

Me: *You can't breathe and feel like you're about to explode.*

Nathan: *Yeah, it's awful. I'm so anxious about work.*

Me: *Got it. Work is causing the shortness of breath and explosion feelings?*

Nathan: *Yes. I really need this job, and I'm terrified I'm going to get fired.*

Me: *You're fearful about getting fired?*

Nathan: *I have this huge presentation due on Friday and I've had NO time to work on it and if I don't get it done then I know they're going to fire me and then I don't know what I'm going to do.*

As soon as Nathan said, "I'm so anxious about work," he identified an origin source, which turned his *general anxiety* into a *specific fear*. The next task was to take the *fear* and turn it into a *worry*.

How to Turn Anxiety into Worry

As we break down Nathan's session, you'll see the path from anxiety to fear to worry—and why it mattered.

WHAT HE SAID	WHAT IT MEANT	INTERVENTION	OUTCOME
"I'm having an anxiety attack."	Unknown. "Anxiety attack" is too general to pinpoint solutions.	Ask clarifying questions.	Nathan identified work as the origin of his feelings.
"I'm so anxious about work."	When Nathan identified the stressor, his general anxiety turned into specific fear.	We needed more clarification; "work" was still too vague to identify an intervention.	Nathan identified specific work factors causing his distress.
"I'm terrified I'm going to get fired."	Once Nathan identified fear of losing his job, we could *then* find a solution.	Reflective listening to elicit more information.	Nathan shrank down his unspecified "work" fear into fear of a specific *outcome*.
"I have this huge presentation due on Friday and I've had NO time to work on it."	Now that Nathan moved from "anxiety attack" to "I have a presentation and no time," we could access solutions.	Nathan realized he could ask for help with childcare, skip out on happy hour, and reschedule meetings.	Nathan left my office with low-key worry rather than high-octane anxiety.

What If I Don't Know the Origin?

If you cannot identify a source of your uncomfortable body sensations, you don't need to go under hypnosis or search for childhood trauma memories. Sometimes all that's needed to lessen anxiety responses is to remind yourself, "My brain is on my side. I don't know why it's feeling threatened, but it's not trying to hurt me." Instead of beating yourself up about why you feel anxious, ask yourself, "What are three people, places, or things available to me *right now* that can help me feel a little bit safer?"

Whether you're feeling anxiety, fear, or worry, remind yourself (at frequent intervals) you are not crazy,* lazy, or broken. When we talk about symptoms without considering context, it places the problem inside *people* rather than on environmental stressors, lack of access to resources, or oppressive systems. Can anxiety/fear/worry feel debilitating and even life-threatening? Without a doubt. Are there times when life renders us powerless? Yes. Nevertheless, anxiety is not a disease—it is an often annoying, sometimes frightening, but always well-meaning part of your internal team.†

The Parts of Your Brain

Just like your mind is made of parts, your physical brain also contains parts, all of which play a wide variety of roles. Think of your brain like a large company with different teams, each with a range of roles and responsibilities, and all of whom share a limited pool of resources.

---

* *Crazy* is a useful word to describe our personal experience, but it is not a clinical term. All symptoms make sense in context, and there is no such thing as a crazy person.

† For Harry Potter enthusiasts, think of anxiety like the Dobby of your brain. It wants to help, but it often causes more harm than good in its efforts.

Disclaimer: The following explanations are intentionally reductive and simplified.

Neocortex (the thinkers): Your neocortex team is responsible for logic, decision-making, risk management, and strategy. Picture a group of executives sitting around a penthouse conference table talking about how the company *should* run and what things *should* qualify as threats. But on all the floors below the neocortex, you have other teams with their own ideas and strategies. This is why you can logically know what you should do but still find yourself doing the exact opposite. If the neocortex thinks you should go to the gym, but there's another team who thinks you need to conserve energy to survive a famine, you'll experience these opposing agendas as procrastination.

When you're mindfused with your thinking team, you may experience overthinking, rumination, and indecisiveness.

Limbic System* (the feelers): A key player on this team is your amygdala—a small, almond-shaped structure in your temporal lobe. Your amygdala is like the panic button of the brain. When it perceives any type of threat, it dispatches a flood of stress hormones to help you survive. People often describe high-intensity emotions as an "amygdala hijack," but your amygdala isn't a terrorist—it's your loyal bodyguard. Though sometimes it seems like your amygdala is tormenting you with its constant cries for help, its intentions are always good. Your amygdala wants to keep you safe—it doesn't hijack your brain, though you'll admittedly feel terrible when it sends stress hormones careening through your body.

When you're mindfused with your feelings team, you may experience emotional reactivity, panic, or shutdown.

---

* The limbic system is not an empirically proven fact—it is a functional concept.

Basal Ganglia (the doers): This team is responsible for automating your movements, so you don't have to think about how to ride a bike, catch a ball, or drive a car once you've learned how to do it. With some of your daily activities automated, you conserve valuable energy for more complex tasks. Your basal ganglia's autopilot setting is why it's hard to break bad habits. If you want to "just stop" doing something you've been used to doing, you need to first switch your autopilot setting to manual. How? The best way to deactivate autopilot is to change up the order of your day. Make your brain work harder. Take different roads to work, change up your morning routine, and listen to different music. *Anything* you do that diverges from your usual will help your brain switch from autopilot to manual. The manual setting is the optimal condition for changing habits.

When you're mindfused with your doer team, you may feel like you're in a trance or watching yourself go through the motions.

Cerebellum (the balancers): This team is responsible for motor coordination and movement control. Whether you are running, jumping, playing sports, or dancing, this part of your brain fine-tunes your movements and tries to prevent stumbles or falls. You can think of these parts of your brain as your in-house physical therapists who are there to help coordinate body actions. When you're overloaded with thoughts and emotions, focusing your attention on your body or getting your body up and moving (to whatever degree you're able) can help.

When you're mindfused with your balancer team, you may hyperfocus on fitness, your body, or the refinement of certain physical activities.

Brain Stem (the life-support team): This team focuses on basic life functions such as breathing, heart rate, reflexes, and digestion. Even when you're asleep, your life-support team is on the job, making sure you stay alive. Your brain stem does not recognize nuance, nor does it care about what's healthy, ethical, or optimal. This part of your brain has only two settings—safety and danger. *Anything* you do that results in you staying alive gets registered as good, even if the behavior is harmful, toxic, or in direct opposition to your values.

When you're mindfused with your life-support team, you can feel reactive and impulsive—like you're no longer yourself.

Sometimes it feels like your brain is a jerk. Comedian Pete Holmes put it best: "Your brain could make you happy all of the time, for no reason whatsoever. Any moment it wants to. It has all the ingredients—dopamine, adrenaline, endorphins. It's all up there. Your brain has the good stuff sequestered in the corner like, 'You want to feel good? You want to feel real nice? *Go for a jog.*'"

Grrr.

Even though it doesn't always make you feel good, your brain is always on your side.* If it thinks you are in danger for any reason (even if you don't think you should feel threatened), it will fuse with one of the four survival parts—fight, flight, freeze, and fawn.

The Four Survival Parts

Long before we developed the capacity to create things like literature, politics, and Snuggies, human brains focused all energy on survival. Your survival parts are primal, hardwired reflexes that allowed your ancestors to survive harsh conditions and wild animals. There are four main survival parts: fight, flight, freeze, and fawn. When you fuse with any

---

* This statement does not include medical complications like dementia or schizophrenia.

of these survival parts, you enter a kablooey state. Using the lion example from earlier:

Fight: When the lion comes through the restaurant, blood rushes to your arms and legs. You spring into action and try to take it down with your salad fork. Other signs of being fused with your fight parts include:

- Aggressive behavior, yelling
- Elevated heart rate, flushed face, clenched fists, tension
- Difficulty listening
- Argumentativeness
- Tunnel vision
- Emotional reactivity

Flight: When you see the lion, you bolt from the table and run into the kitchen to hide. Other signs of being fused with your flight parts include:

- Avoidance of confrontation
- Restlessness or fidgeting
- Difficulty concentrating
- Racing thoughts
- Distractedness
- Scanning the room looking for the exit
- Sweating, shaking, tingling

Freeze: When the lion stares you down, your body tenses up, your breath slows, and you find yourself unable to move, think, or speak. Other signs of being fused with your freeze parts include:

- Indecisiveness
- Immobility (feeling glued to your couch or screen)
- Dissociation, spacing out, glazed eyes

- Slowed speech, delayed responses
- Disconnection from body
- Sense of nonreality

Fawn: When you see the lion, you invite it to sit down, tell it how wonderful it is, and offer to give it your sandwich, even though you were hungry only moments earlier. This response is also known as the people-pleasing response. Other signs of being fused with your fawn parts include:

- Not setting boundaries
- Overapologizing
- Being excessively polite
- Avoiding conflict by agreeing
- Seeking constant reassurance
- Prioritizing someone's needs over your own
- Feeling guilty for saying no

In Nathan's case earlier in this chapter, he came into his session fused with his freeze parts—he couldn't breathe, feel his body, or think of any of his considerable list of resources. When he defused from his freeze response, his "thinking parts" came back to the table.

Why do some people fight, but others people-please? Why do you freeze up at work but run away from intimacy? Survival responses are unconscious and automatic; you don't get to vote for your favorite. None of the survival responses are inherently good or bad, nor are they an indicator of strength, character, or bravery. Your brain's responses are a combination of environment, genetics, past experiences, and the nature of the situation. Regardless of which one shows up, all four options exist for one purpose—to enhance your survival odds.*

---

* Children often default to the freeze response, since there's no chance of them winning a fight and nowhere for them to flee.

What Do Survival Parts Have to Do
with Shifting from Mindfused to Mindful?

You can't move from mindfused to mindful while your brain is locked in a survival state. If you were in the middle of prepping a meal and your stove caught on fire, you'd immediately drop everything and try to put the fire out. Despite your *Top Chef*–worthy knife skills, in that moment you wouldn't remember how to julienne the carrots—nor would you care. When your stove goes up in flames, your brain shifts into emergency mode over *everything* else. Even though life's lions and fires are not always as obvious as the one in the preceding stories, your brain is always trying to help you stay alive. Later in this book you'll learn to work with your inner critic, your impulsive parts, and your impostor parts, but before you can develop a harmonious relationship with your psychological parts, you'll need to first defuse from your brain's physiological parts. This is a process called *emotional regulation*. Emotional regulation is a clinical way of saying, "Switch your brain settings from lion to logic."

Disclaimer: There are no brain hacks, mindfulness tools, or coping skills that will make an unsafe situation safe. Sometimes, when "doing the work" doesn't get you anywhere, it isn't because you aren't trying hard enough, it's because you aren't *safe* enough. Occasionally our brains misinterpret danger cues in the environment and create unnecessary symptoms, but often our inability to feel better makes total sense in context.

How to Defuse from Survival Brain

When you're mindfused with your brain's survival parts, thinking strategies often fail to work. This isn't because there's anything wrong with you or your mind. Positive thinking and affirmations often fall flat because *physical problems* need *physical solutions*. Assuming you are in a safe enough situation with access to resources and choices, you can use the acronym DEFUSE when you're stuck in a state of fight, flight, freeze, or fawn:

D: Describe your physical sensations.

E: Exit the room.

F: Feel your body.

U: Use your senses.

S: Shift.

E: Exhale.*

Here's how this works:

Describe your physical sensations: It's easy to get stuck on unhelpful thought loops when parts get activated. The first step to defusing from a survival state is to ignore your thoughts and instead describe your *body sensations*. For example, "I'm feeling tightness in my chest, tension in my jaw, sweat on my palms, stomach cramps, and tingling in my feet."

Exit the room: When you get stuck in survival brain, leave the room, or move to another location if you're outside. Physically leaving the space (even if you're perfectly safe) can help your brain recognize you've successfully "escaped."

Feel your body: You can gently tap your face, rub your hands together, massage your calves, or squeeze your toes. Physically feeling different areas of your body helps your brain to recognize safety.

Use your senses: The 5-4-3-2-1 method is a popular method of using senses to deactivate survival brain states. Notice five things you can see, four things you can touch, three things you can hear, two things you can smell, and one thing you can taste.

---

* There are times when breath work is problematic for your nervous system. This is a thing. If counting/forcing breaths doesn't work, don't do it.

Shift: Shifting your body is an effective way to defuse. Shaking your arms and legs, stomping your feet on the ground, and shoving heavy furniture around can help your brain to align with safety. Putting on music and dancing gives you double bang for your buck, since music is sensory, and dancing shifts your physical body.

Exhale: When you exhale longer than you inhale, you engage your brain's relaxation response. Long exhalations cue your nervous system to switch out of survival mode into a more mindful state. One way to do this is by doing a 1:2 breathing ratio. Count how many seconds you breathe in through your nose, then exhale slowly through your mouth for twice that time. If you count two seconds in through your nose, then exhale through your mouth while counting to four. If you count four seconds in through your nose, exhale through your mouth while counting to eight.

Defusing Does Not Equal Calmness

Knowing how to defuse from survival parts is the single most powerful skill in the world of parts work. But defusing from your brain's survival responses isn't about maintaining a sense of calm—it's about maintaining a sense of *choice*.

- You can be defused and angry.
- You can be defused and sad.
- You can be defused and scared.
- You can be defused and stressed.

The wellness world often hails calmness as the ultimate status symbol, but feeling perfectly balanced and calm is overrated. There are two types of stress, only one of which is problematic.

The Two Types of Stress

Just as there are two types of cholesterol, HDL (good) and LDL (bad), there are two types of stress—**distress** and **eustress**. *Distress* is the "bad" stress. It eats away at your well-being and reduces the quality of your life. *Eustress* is the "good" stress. It's the HDL stress of your system. Eustress is your get-up-and-go juice, and it enhances your life. If you want to go for a run, improve your career skills, or try a new hobby, you'll need eustress. Defusing allows you to stay in the driver's seat of your brain—it is *not* intended to eliminate tension and stress.

The goal of parts work is to feel *empowered,* not to feel calm. When we aim for calmness instead of truth, we create an internal split. As writer and philosopher Aldous Huxley put it, "Too much tension is a disease; but so is too little. There are certain occasions when we ought to be tense, when an excess of tranquility (and especially of tranquility imposed from the outside, by a chemical) is entirely inappropriate." Living with zero stress would be like sitting in a car with no gas—you're not going to get very far. Trauma pioneer Peter Levine wrote in *Waking the Tiger*: "In order to stay healthy, our nervous systems and psyches need to face challenges and to succeed in meeting those challenges."

Conclusion

Internal diversity is as important to your well-being as biodiversity is to the environment. You might not personally enjoy possums or spiders, but nature needs their contributions. Without a diverse mix of animals, plant species, and microbes, entire ecosystems collapse. We don't struggle because of internal *diversity*—we struggle because of internal *fusion*. When you defuse, you get immediate relief from panic, shutdown, indecision, stress, and worry. Your external world may not get easier, but when you're unfused, you can navigate it better. When your brain *brains* better, life gets better. Learning to defuse is more effective than trying to ignore your thoughts or eliminate your parts. You don't need to get rid of any of your parts. To experience wholeness and happiness, we need *all* our parts to play their diverse roles—even the parts you don't like, which are called *shadow parts*. The next chapter will show you how to unlock the powerful gifts contained within each of your shadow parts.

Bottom-Line Takeaways

1. Your brain is on your side—even when it's doing peculiar things.

2. *Mind fusion* is like nuclear fusion—when parts fuse together . . . kablooey.

3. The opposite of mindfused is mindful.

4. *Defusing* is the path that leads from mindfused to mindful.

5. Mindfulness is more than mindset—it's also a physiological state.

6. Anxiety is not created in your mind—it's created in your body.

7. Just as your mind is made of parts, your brain is also made of parts.

8. When you're mindfused with survival brain, you'll go into fight, flight, freeze, or fawn.

9. To defuse from survival brain, use the acronym DEFUSE (describe your physical sensations, exit

the room, feel your body, use your senses, shift, exhale longer than you inhale).

10. The goal of defusing is not to create a sense of calm—it's to create a sense of choice.

Action Step Options

I have no time (1–5 minutes):
DEFUSE.

Set a timer for 5 minutes. Try all of the six tasks of the DE-FUSE acronym:

1. Describe your physical sensations.
2. Exit the room.
3. Feel your body.
4. Use your senses.
5. Shift.
6. Exhale longer than you inhale.

I have some time (5–15 minutes):
Track your DEFUSE progress.

Copy the chart into your journal or notebook, and jot down your results:

Task	Results: What did you experience? What did you do? How did it work?	On a scale of 1 to 10, how defused do you feel?
Describe your physical sensations.		
Exit the room.		
Feel your body.		
Use your senses.		
Shift.		
Exhale longer than you inhale.		

I'll make time (15–45 minutes):

Do the first two exercises, then answer the following three journal prompts:

1. Who are the people, where are the places, and what are some things that can help me move from mind-fused to mindful? Where do I feel the safest/most seen/most connected?

2. When was the last time I felt most like myself (or the closest to how I'd like to feel)?

3. Who/what/where are my triggers for mind fusion? How can I use my resources (people/places/things) to help prevent me from going into survival mode?

Chapter 3

Shadow Work

The Gifts of Hidden Parts

Skipping Shadow Work is like skipping "Leg Day."
—**Martin O'Toole**, *How to Die Happy*

In one of the most shocking performance art exhibitions of all time, Marina Abramović exposed a chilling truth— ordinary people have the capacity to cause extraordinary harm. During her controversial 1970s performance piece *Rhythm 0*, Abramović stood silent and still for six hours near a table piled with an assortment of objects. The objects ranged from harmless things like perfume, flowers, and honey to more sinister tools including chains, knives, and a gun. Accompanying the items was a note:

Instructions
There are 72 objects on the table that
one can use on me as desired.

Performance
I am the object.
During this period I take full responsibility.

Initially, people responded with tame curiosity. They offered her flowers and gently fed her fruit. But emboldened by the consequence-free environment, the group quickly descended into an aggressive mob. The details of what ensued are too gruesome to describe here, but you can google it if you want the full account. One audience member went so far as to hold a loaded gun to her head and force her finger around the trigger, stopping only when a concerned bystander intervened. True to her word, Abramović stood silently for the entire ordeal, tears in her eyes as she endured horrific treatment. At the end of the six-hour period, her body pushed to the brink, she stopped the performance by simply walking toward the audience. Terrified by the sudden prospect of confrontation, everyone fled from the room.*

Why share this story?

Famed Russian novelist Fyodor Dostoevsky wrote, "Nothing is easier than to denounce the evildoer; nothing is more difficult than to understand him." It's easy to scoff at extreme behavior and say, "Well, I would *never* do anything like that. I'm a good person." But Abramović's work proved *good* and *evil* are not binary categories into which people neatly fall. *Rhythm 0* didn't take place deep in the woods or in a cult leader's secret basement. The entire spectacle unfolded in a brightly lit Naples studio filled with art patrons—people who read books and baked cookies; people who sang to their babies and paid bills. The audience wasn't a group of notorious criminals on a field trip, and it's statistically impossible that every single attendee was an undiagnosed sociopath.

Nevertheless, Abramović nearly died during her performance.

Rhythm 0 showed *everyone*—you, me, your sweet elderly neighbor, and your favorite elementary school teacher—comes installed with a full set of human qualities. Not all

---

* The photographs documenting this performance are disturbing and eye-opening. If there were ever any doubts about the existence of psychological shadows, *Rhythm 0* does a bang-up job obliterating them.

people act out every impulse, but embedded in the human psyche is the potential for the highest highs—and the lowest lows. We exist in a world of opposites—night and day, sun and moon, up and down, fire and ice, life and death. Our minds are the same. Anthony Burgess, author of *A Clockwork Orange,* said it best when he wrote, "It is as inhuman to be totally good as it is to be totally evil."

Now, I realize it's unlikely you'll ever physically harm another person or participate in criminally antisocial behavior. But as you read in chapter 1, your mind contains a multitude of parts. Some of these parts are kind, generous, and giving. Others are more difficult to acknowledge. From early childhood we're taught to split the world into the good guys and the bad guys. This internal split is why we end up shocked when "good" people do bad things. But there's not a neat and clean divide of *us* versus *them* when it comes to humaning. We *all* have parts we dislike, parts we fear, and parts we go to great lengths to avoid. These are called *shadow parts*.

One important aspect of parts work is to cultivate a relationship with your shadow parts instead of fighting with or feeling controlled by them. Famed Swiss psychiatrist, author, and founder of analytical psychology Carl Jung put it this way: "People will do anything, no matter how absurd, in order to avoid facing their own soul. One does not become enlightened by imagining figures of light, but by making the darkness conscious. The latter procedure, however, is disagreeable and therefore not popular."

The unpopular "latter procedure" Jung referred to is called *shadow work*.

What Is Shadow Work?

The term *shadow* sounds super woo-woo, but the concept is simple. All physical objects cast shadows. If you put your hand up toward your ceiling light, you'll see a shadow of your hand on the wall. Physical shadows form any time light is blocked. Psychological shadows form any time awareness is blocked. *Shadow parts* are any aspects of your inner world who exist outside your conscious awareness. *Shadow work* is the process of both recognizing these exiled parts and welcoming them home. There's a common misconception that shadow work is only about toxic, damaging, and negative aspects of the human psyche, but shadows are morally neutral—your shadow is made of *any* aspects outside your awareness, including qualities like confidence and enthusiasm. Shadows are often tame and sometimes even positive. I define shadow work like this:

> *Shadow work is the process of getting honest **with** yourself **about** yourself without **shaming** yourself.*

The distance between your authentic Self and the person you think you *should* be is the measure of your shadow. The greater the gap, the larger your shadow. In this chapter, you'll learn how your shadow parts formed, why they matter, and how you can find and connect with them. But don't worry—this information is not designed to shame you and it won't be a total downer. Not all aspects of your shadow are negative or undesirable. Shadow work exposes the not-so-nice corners of the human mind, but it also uncovers hidden gems.

Rhythm 0 demonstrated the presence of negative shadows, but in this chapter, we'll also talk about the concept of *golden shadows,* a term popularized by Jungian analyst and prolific author Robert A. Johnson. Golden shadows are undeveloped or unrecognized positive qualities. These qualities are equally if not more likely to go into the shadow. Johnson observed, "Curiously, people resist the noble aspects of their shadows more strenuously than they hide the [negative] sides. To draw the skeletons out of the closet is relatively easy, but to own the gold in the shadow is terrifying."

It's puzzling to think good qualities could pose problems. Many people hear about golden shadows and say, "*Of course* I want access to my untapped strengths and hidden talents— who *wouldn't* want that?"

But your brain is designed to keep you alive, *not* to make you happy. Brains prefer the predictability of patterns— healthy or not. All change, even positive change, can register in your brain as dangerous. From a neuroscience perspective, golden shadows are terribly disruptive to your brain, despite their valuable offerings. You may not enjoy the feeling of being stuck, but there are benefits to staying exactly where you are, who you are, and how you operate. When you reconnect with golden shadows and build an inner empire of health, wealth, wisdom, and happiness, you're guaranteed to disturb dormant shadows in the people around you. Misery loves company, but happiness can initially feel lonely. Personal growth almost always requires a shedding of people for whom your uplevel is threatening.

Shadow work can sound daunting, but when you remember your mind is made of parts, it's way less scary to fish around in your unconscious. If qualities like envy and resentment are not who you are but simply a *part* of who you are, it is easier to get curious about them. When you realize your desire for internet popularity is a *part* of you (and doesn't immediately brand you a narcissist), you're less likely to go blank when it's time to create content. Not all behaviors are acceptable, but as Internal Family Systems creator Dr. Richard Schwartz teaches, "all parts are welcome." You don't need to fear *any* aspects of your shadow—positive or negative—when they're simply a *part* of who you are, not the totality of your being.

A Caution About Shadow Work

Before you try to connect with *any* parts of your mind, it is important you're in a safe enough environment with access to resources and your basic needs met. When you're not safe, shadow work is neither necessary nor helpful. If you struggle with mental health symptoms of any kind, shadow work can trigger these symptoms and make them worse. Sometimes people jump straight to shadow work when what is first needed is *trauma* work. As you read through these pages, if at any point you find yourself flooded or distressed, skip this chapter and return to it with the help of a trained mental health professional. If you don't have access to a trained mental health professional, bookmark this chapter for future reference.

Why Do Shadow Work?

When you reconnect with your shadow parts, you unlock their important messages and powerful gifts. These neglected aspects of yourself carry valuable insights and lessons that can enrich your life. As you acknowledge and accept these parts, the energy consumed by suppressing or denying them releases. Even though shadow work is a psychological process, it comes with physical benefits. When you're no longer burning energy running away from your mind, you'll feel more vibrant and alive.

There's not one molecule of your being who isn't precious, valuable, and important. You are not a mistake, and neither are your shadow parts. If you feel resistant to your shadow parts as you work through these pages, remind yourself of this powerful truth:

No one needs to know what you discover about yourself unless you choose to share.

Frankly, if everyone held a microphone to their minds and we could all hear one another's thoughts, society would collapse. Thankfully, thoughts are private. In J. M. Barrie's classic tale *Peter Pan*, Peter reassures his frightened shadow by reminding it, "You needn't be so scared. No one will ever see us but ourselves."

How Shadows Form

Shadows can form at any stage of life, but early childhood is a fertile soil for shadow growth, unless you had the great fortune to grow up with caregivers who honored your divergence from family norms. Even well-intentioned parents often lack the skills to hold compassionate space for their children's complex development. All families—even relatively healthy families—have different blueprints for socially acceptable behavior, and children quickly learn to adapt. If children fail to follow the unwritten family rules, they risk abandonment and rejection by their caregivers. Since kids have no money, power, or viable escape route, abandonment or rejection by caregivers is tantamount to death. Examples of unwritten family rules include:

- You can trust only your family.
- If you don't finish all the food on your plate, you're ungrateful.
- You should never question adults.
- Do as I say, not as I do.
- Don't think, don't speak, don't feel.
- Don't air the family's dirty laundry.
- Boys don't cry.
- Girls should be sweet.
- Children should be seen and not heard.

If you grew up in a family with the unwritten rule "It's not nice to feel angry," your angry parts had to hide. As an adult, you may find yourself constantly worn out by people-pleasing and operating from the "go along to get along" mentality. Until you reconnect with your angry parts, you'll feel ashamed and guilty any time angry feelings dare to surface. In my case, my caregivers wielded anger freely (and explosively) but rejected all the other feelings. Instead of developing an anger shadow, I developed a sensitivity shadow—all my deeply feeling parts went into exile until I learned how to bring them home. There are countless shadow varietals, but the seven most common are as follows.

Seven Types of Shadows

1. Personal shadows

Personal shadows are your specific personality traits, emotions, desires, and qualities. These may include aspects of your inner world that you think are unacceptable or shameful, such as greed, envy, or unhappiness. Toxic positivity is an indicator that personal shadow work is needed.

Someone with a personal shadow might say, "I'm grateful for everything in my life all the time."

2. Family shadows

Family shadows are inherited patterns, beliefs, and behaviors passed down through generations within both sides of a family system. These may include unresolved conflicts, family secrets, and dysfunctional dynamics. The past does not stay in the past. The past stays present until it's processed, which is why family secrets keep families sick. Refusing to discuss family history is an indicator that family shadow work is needed.

Someone with a family shadow might say, "In this family, we don't talk about the past."

3. Cultural shadows

Cultural shadows include biases, unspoken rules, taboos, or patterns of treating people. Cultural shadows include racism, stereotypical gender roles, or monogamy as the only "right" way to be in an intimate relationship. Refusing to acknowledge biases or prejudices is an indicator that cultural shadow work is needed.

Someone with a cultural shadow might say, "There's no such thing as privilege."

4. Creativity shadows

Everyone is creative, but creativity shadows hold us back from fully expressing creative potential. Creativity shadows can come from past experiences, such as being criticized for ideas or feeling insecure about a perceived lack of talent. If you wanted to be a singer but grew up in a family who insisted you practice law, you may feel judgmental toward creative people and avoid the arts altogether. If you ever doubt your creativity or hold yourself back because you fear failure, it's likely a creativity shadow is lurking in the corner.

Someone with a creativity shadow might say, "Making art is a waste of time."

5. Trauma shadows

Trauma shadows are the result of trauma-inflicted injuries that have gone untended. The human nervous system stores all experiences, and if we don't address traumatic injuries, they can show up as unexplained emotional outbursts or physical symptoms.* Sometimes environmental or systemic factors make this task impossible, but until a traumatic injury is brought to conscious awareness, unconscious patterns perpetuate.

---

* Always go to a medical doctor to rule out medical causes of a symptom before assuming it has psychological origins.

Someone with a trauma shadow might say, "Well, yeah, that terrible thing happened. But doesn't every kid deserve that treatment?"

6. Relationship shadows

Relationship shadows are problematic patterns of behavior or dynamics in a relationship that neither person wants to admit. Friendships or intimate relationships where abuse or active addiction is present often cast relationship shadows.

Someone with a relationship shadow might worry about their partner's drinking habits but say to themselves and others, "Everyone indulges. What harm does it really do?"

7. Financial shadows

Financial shadows refer to repressed or denied aspects of your relationship with money. This may include overspending, chronic underearning, feeling at war with money, or disconnecting from the reality of your finances. Financial shadows manifest themselves in refusing to budget, hoarding, not buying necessities like toilet paper or going to the doctor even when you have the money, or feeling guilty for wanting more money and resentful toward people who have more money than you.

Someone with a financial shadow might say, "Rich people are all greedy and selfish."

Shadows develop because your brain's first job is to preserve life—not to expand consciousness. When parts are faced with rejection from family, culture, or society, they have no choice but to retreat. Once safely confined to the edges of your unconscious, shadow parts are then guarded by fierce protectors who go to great lengths to keep you away. If the concept of cowering shadow parts and sword-wielding protector parts sounds a bit melodramatic, let's look at a real-life example:

Cady, twenty-seven, came to therapy because during her birthday month each April, she experienced severe panic episodes. Frustrated by yet another yearly visit to the ER, she decided it was time to figure out what was causing the clockwork panic cycle. Cady grew up in a high-control fundamentalist religious community, where she was required to give away all her toys and never ask for or complain about anything. As we worked together, Cady recalled a memory of asking her mother for a skateboard to celebrate her tenth birthday. Disgusted, her mother chastised the little girl: "How dare you. There are children who live without food or a safe place to live. You should be ashamed of yourself for not being more grateful."

After that incident, Cady never asked for another birthday gift (or for anything at all). Since the quality of wanting was forbidden by her family and her community, all of Cady's desires stayed safely confined to her shadow. When Cady reached adulthood and her well-meaning friends asked her what she wanted for her birthday, her protector parts sprang into action, creating intense panic. If you could peek inside Cady's mind in the style of Pixar's *Inside Out*, you might hear something like this:

Shadow Part: "OOOO, it's our birthday! Maybe this year it would be okay to want something? After all, our friends asked us to tell them what we wanted. It sure would be nice to have a birthday party with maybe just a few *small* gifts."

Protector Part: "Oh no! She's about to want something! That's against the rules. This is a dangerous situation, team. Wanting something will result in death. Quick! Hit the panic button so she'll forget to want anything!"

Parts may live in your mind, but they create very real sensations in your body. If you've ever felt drowsy during meditation, distracted when you try to journal, or fidgety when you forget your headphones, that's a sign your protector parts are on high alert.* When shadow parts venture too close to conscious awareness, protective parts tend to get jumpy. But when you defuse from protector parts (see chapter 2), you can then safely reconnect with shadow parts without sending your system into a state of fight, flight, freeze, or fawn. We'll talk more about protector parts in chapters 4 and 5.

Why Shadow Work Matters

Carl Jung wrote, "Until you make the unconscious conscious, it will direct your life and you will call it fate." If you want to feel in charge of your life, in control of your choices, and responsive to stressors rather than reactive to triggers, you need to have access to *all* your parts.† Some people think you should banish certain parts and keep only the ones who "spark joy." But while you can declutter your physical space à la Marie Kondo by donating or giving away your stuff, you cannot get rid of or rehome your parts—nor will you ever want to once you get to know them. Happiness requires wholeness, and wholeness requires connection with *every* aspect of your mind. It takes a tremendous amount of energy to suppress authenticity. When your protector parts are on guard, your motivation tank drains. Shadow work frees up your energy so you can use it for other things.

Other benefits of shadow work include:

- Feeling more like yourself

---

* It could also be a sign that you're tired, hungry, or coming down with the flu. Not every symptom suggests a deep-rooted psychological phenomenon.

† This sentiment assumes you have solved for safety. Feeling in charge of your life requires you to have a safe enough environment and access to resources.

- Emotional healing
- Inner alignment
- Access to creativity and flow
- Increased energy
- Personal growth
- Freedom from limiting beliefs
- Stress reduction
- Better relationships

When we seek goodness at the expense of wholeness, our shadow parts tend to rebel and either act outward or collapse inward. Your openness and willingness to accommodate your shadow parts is what I call *shadow intelligence*. If emotional intelligence (EQ) is the measure of emotional awareness, and one's intelligence quotient (IQ) is the measure of logic and reasoning abilities, shadow intelligence (SQ) is the degree to which you're connected to and in alignment with all your parts.

INTELLIGENCE TYPE	WHAT IT IS
Emotional intelligence (EQ)	The ability to maintain awareness and control over your emotions and the skills to understand, manage, and express them appropriately. This includes empathy, self-regulation, social skills, and self-awareness.
Intelligence quotient (IQ)	A score derived from standardized tests designed to measure cognitive abilities such as reasoning, problem-solving, abstract thinking, and memory.
Shadow intelligence (SQ)	The ability to maintain awareness of and connection with all aspects of your mind, including the parts you don't particularly like.

The higher your shadow intelligence (SQ), the more at home you'll feel in your mind and in your body. Living your best life does not require the absence of parts, but the presence of Self. Seeress and healer Deborah Hanekamp, better known by her moniker, Mama Medicine, wrote, "For how can we really discover our Original Essence if we are only interested in seeing the parts of ourselves we are proud of?" Or as Rupi Kaur put it, "It was when I stopped searching for home within others and lifted the foundations of home within myself I found there were no roots more intimate than those between a mind and body that have decided to be whole."

How to Do Shadow Work in Three Steps

The first step to building shadow intelligence is to admit you have shadow parts—even if you're unsure who they are or where to find them. If there were a first step to shadow work, it would be: "We admitted we have shadow parts, and as a result of ignoring them, life is less than ideal." After you've validated the existence of your shadow parts, the next steps are to defuse from protector parts, ferret out hidden parts, and then initiate a process of reconnection. More simply put, the three steps to shadow work are:

1. Regulate   2. Excavate   3. Activate

Step One: Regulate

When your nervous system is in protective mode, your brain shifts from emotional regulation to emotional *dysregulation*, more commonly known as fight, flight, freeze, or fawn. If you're fused with the parts of your brain responsible for survival, it will be nearly impossible to find or connect with any other parts until you defuse and regulate. To do this, use the DEFUSE acronym from chapter 2:

D: Describe your physical sensations.

E: Exit the room.

F: Feel your body.

U: Use your senses.

S: Shift.

E: Exhale.

Once you've completed the defusing process, check in with yourself to see how open and curious you feel toward your parts. Then say to your mind, "Hi, everyone. Do I have permission to go inside and talk to shadow parts today?" (If this sounds bizarre, that's because it *is*.) Even though we all talk to ourselves daily, dialoguing with your mind can feel wacky and uncomfortable. But remember—no one is listening to your thoughts but you. If you ask for permission and then listen carefully to your mind for an answer, you'll sense a yes or a no from your internal system. If you hear no, repeat the first step and then check again.

Regulation doesn't always produce calmness, but when you're in a regulated state you'll be able to consider options and make decisions. You'll know you've nailed the regulation step when you feel curious about and open toward your parts. If you feel anxious, judgmental, or disdainful toward any part of yourself, that's an indicator you're still fused with your protector parts.

Regulation Troubleshooting: If you get stuck, take a few minutes to evaluate your current environment. If you're slammed with obligations, burdened with tasks, hungry, tired, or in any way not in a place where it makes sense to slow down, your system is wise to deny you entry. You can ask yourself, "What would need to happen right now for me to feel safe and comfortable enough to do this?"

Once you've accessed feelings of curiosity and openness toward your parts, you're safe to proceed with step two.

Step Two: Excavate

Once you feel regulated, the next step is to coax your shadow parts out of hiding. A common objection I hear at this point of the process is: "But how am I supposed to find my shadow parts if I don't know who they are or where they live?" Fair question. Fortunately, once you know where to look, you'll discover a national park's worth of trails leading to shadow parts. The following five trailheads might not all be relevant to you, so skim the list and work through the ones that resonate.

Five Places Your Shadow Parts Hide

1. Childhood Ambitions

Do you remember what you wanted to be when you grew up? If your younger self plastered pictures of the Galápagos on the wall, pretended to be an Arctic explorer, and dreamed of a life filled with travel and new experiences, but as an adult you haven't wandered outside your zip code in years, your childhood ambitions provide clues to your shadow parts.

How to excavate: Ask yourself, "What did I dream of as a child? How much of that dream is present or absent from my current life?" If there's a laundry list of childhood wishes that have zero presence in your adult life, that's a flashing indicator light pointing toward a shadow part. In the example above, the shadow part might be called "the one who wants to travel."

2. People Who Annoy You

One of the easiest places to find shadow parts is to make a mental list of people who annoy you.* When you get frustrated with your chatty coworker or bothered by your partner's decision to wear Crocs with socks, that's a sign one of your shadow parts is near.

How to excavate: Think of a person who annoys you. Then ask yourself, "What are the qualities about this person that bother me? Is it possible that I could have this quality, too? If your coworker bothers you because she talks too much, you might call your shadow part "the one who talks too much." If your partner's sartorial choices create fear of not being cool, you might call this part "the one who isn't cool."

3. People Who Spark Jealousy

Jealousy is a well-paved path to shadow parts. It has a bad reputation, but it isn't good or bad until you take an action. Jealousy is a wellspring of information about what you want to do, be, or have. Any time the green-eyed gremlin pops up, remind yourself that underneath the "jealousy monster" is a shadow part who wants, needs, and deserves your attention.

How to excavate: Think of an influencer, friend, or public figure who ignites feelings of jealousy. Then ask yourself, "What is it about this person's life that I desire?" The answer leads straight to your shadow part. If you're jealous of an influencer who has a gorgeous home with perfectly arranged decor, your jealousy might indicate the presence of a shadow part who desires more beauty in your surroundings. You might call this part "the one who likes pretty things."

4. Your Favorite Shows

We gravitate toward our favorite shows for different reasons,

---

* This step assumes the person in question is not actively causing harm to you or others.

but your choice of movies, television, and music provides valuable intel on your shadow parts. True crime or prison dramas are among the strongest examples of how shows point toward shadows. Some (not all) people obsess about crime-based shows because of trauma shadows. Dr. Thema Bryant pointed this out in a podcast interview. She said, "If your idea of relaxing before you go to sleep is watching three episodes of *Law & Order*, I would encourage you to think about, 'Why is trauma relaxing to me?'"

How to excavate: Make a list or think of all your favorite movies and shows. Look for themes. If your favorite movies are *The Avengers*, *Thor*, *Spider-Man*, and *Ready Player One*, you may have a hero hiding in your shadow. You might call this part "the one who wants to save the day." If your favorite shows and podcasts are all about courtroom drama, you might call your shadow part "the one who demands justice."

5. Celebrities You Admire

One of the easiest ways to find golden shadow parts is by looking at your favorite celebrity. Celebrity culture is so wildly pervasive, there's even a psychological assessment called the Celebrity Attitude Scale to evaluate the psychological health of someone's interest (from mild curiosity to stalker obsession) in their favorite celebrity. "Post-concert depression" is a phenomenon associated with Taylor Swift's 2023 Eras Tour, but you can look at any celebrity fan base throughout history and see people faint, scream, or go deep into financial debt to attend concerts. Whether you subscribe to it or not, celebrity culture is here to stay, so we might as well put it to good use by mining it for shadow content.

How to excavate: Think of your favorite celebrity. What are the qualities about this person you most admire? What qualities do you think they have but you lack? These are the qualities hiding in your golden shadow. You might call this part "the one who is talented" or "the one who is powerful."

Excavation troubleshooting: If you looked at all five areas and are unable to locate a shadow part, return to the regulation step and again ask for permission from your mind before proceeding. You can say to yourself, "Hi, parts. I see that you're not really interested in letting me go inside right now. What do you need to feel safe enough to allow me access?" Listen for an answer, then return to the list of hiding places.

Once you've uncovered a part (or group of parts), choose one with whom you'd like to work and then proceed to step three.

Step Three: Activate

Now that you've regulated your nervous system and identified a shadow part, it's time to activate the reconnection process. If you haven't guessed by now, I'm a fan of acronyms. The one I use for step three is **ALIGN**: Acknowledge, Listen, Investigate, Give Gratitude, Negotiate.

How to ALIGN

You can read through the acronym and do the steps in your head, but parts work tends to go faster and be more effective when you write things down. Old-school pen and paper writing works best with your brain's design, but you can also use the Notes app or something similar on your phone. Digital parts work is preferable to none. You can use the "what to do" prompts exactly as written, or you can use them as a guide and come up with words of your own. I'll first break down all the aspects of ALIGN, then walk you through a specific example.

A: Acknowledge availability.

If you had a problem and went to a good friend to talk it out, that person (if they were available) would put their phone down, look you in the eye, and communicate their interest and availability. Your parts need the same level of presence. Trying to work with a shadow part while watching TV or playing a game on your phone communicates a lack of interest. When parts don't feel seen and heard, they either temporarily go quiet or loudly demand attention through less-than-optimal behaviors.

What to do: First, make sure you are available. *Available* means you are both regulated (curious and compassionate toward your parts) and in a distraction-free zone. Turn off your TV or computer, and plan to invest at least a few minutes in this practice. Then say to yourself or write, "Hello, [insert name of part]. I am here for you. I want to help you. For the next five minutes [or however long you choose to allocate to this work] I am available to connect with you."

L: Listen.

It's been said prayer is the act of talking to a higher power and meditation is the act of listening. Listening to parts requires the same muscles as meditating. The temptation for most people when they first meet their parts is to tell them like it is. Someone might discover a shadow part and sternly instruct them, "Stop it. You're safe. There's no reason to feel this way." If you've ever communicated like this with a toddler (or teenager), you'll very quickly learn talking at someone using *your* words is less effective than listening to *theirs*.

What to do: After you've let your part know you're available, say to it or write, "I want to hear everything on your mind." Then listen for a reply. (This may feel mystical and strange, but it's just a different way to think about thinking.) Without judging, shaming, or arguing with the part, simply listen and write down what you hear.

I: Investigate.

Once you've listened to the shadow part, you'll need to gather more information before you make any decisions.

What to do: Ask the part clarifying questions if you're confused about what it needs or wants until you feel confident about the dilemma.

G: Give gratitude.

Most people are familiar with the advice to express gratitude to other people, but expressing gratitude *inward* is just as important. Thanking your part may feel counterintuitive, especially if its presence has caused discomfort or stress. But practicing gratitude inward creates a healthy attachment and a sense of internal trust between you and your parts.

What to do: Consider what this part has tried to do on your behalf. Either think about or write a thank-you note to the part for trying to help you. Just as your physical brain is always on your side and wants to keep you alive, all your parts have the same goal—even when their efforts are unskillful.

*Important disclaimer: Intention does not negate impact, and explanation is not synonymous with excuse. Parts work is about connecting with your parts, not about justifying their behavior. And if two people are in a relationship where both parties are familiar with parts work, it's *wholly unacceptable* for someone to say to you, "Well, my parts are just trying to help me stay alive, so that's why I screamed at you." NO. Parts work is an inside job, and it's never your responsibility to connect with, tend to, or excuse the behavior of someone else's parts.

N: Negotiate.

After acknowledging, listening to, investigating the concerns of your shadow part, and thanking it for its presence, it's time to negotiate. When you approach the inner negotiation table with compassion and an open mind, you and your shadow parts will be able to call a ceasefire. The most important thing to know about this step is negotiation is not about winning—it's about coming to a mutually agreeable solution. As trust grows, your system relaxes, and your parts will require less of your time and attention.

What to do: Start by identifying potential compromises while staying aligned with your overall values and goals. Be willing to explore creative solutions as you consider your resources—what people, places, or things are available to help soothe your part's fear or alleviate its concerns? The more information you have about the specific concerns of the part, the better equipped you'll be to negotiate a solution. I use a negotiation strategy called Shadow Snacks when I do this work. These are conscious indulgences I permit my parts to enjoy. Shadow snacks satisfy my parts without causing any harm to myself or to others. Everyone likes snacks, including shadow parts. Feeding your shadow parts "snacks" might look like:

- Watching horror movies
- Putting on music and dancing
- Taking a nap when you "should" be productive
- Playing with Legos
- Giving yourself permission to stay in your pajamas all day
- Giving yourself permission not to shower
- Letting yourself eat cereal for dinner

*Disclaimer about shadow snacks: Shadow snacks are small, conscious indulgences. They are *not* a hall pass to indulge every impulse.

ALIGN is a tool that you can use with any parts, and we'll revisit the acronym later in this book when we work with impostor parts, critical parts, younger parts, and impulsive parts. Here's a step-by-step example of how to use this strategy with a jealous shadow part.

ALIGN Example: Working with a Jealous Part

Let's say you're scrolling through social media and you see your friend's photos of her tropical vacation. Immediately your stomach lurches, you feel heat behind your neck, and prickly feelings of jealousy mixed with a hint of resentment bubble up to the surface. You immediately feel guilty for having this feeling, but instead of pretending you're *not* jealous or deciding you must be a bad person for feeling jealous, you can ALIGN.

ALIGN Step	What It Sounds Like	What This Does
A: Acknowledge your availability.	"Hi, jealous part. I know you're upset. I'm here and available for you for the next fifteen minutes."	Defuses you from your jealous part. You are not your jealousy, and your jealousy is not you. It is a part of you, and it needs your attention.
L: Listen.	"So, jealous part . . . what are you going through? Help me understand what hurts you and what you need."	Listening allows your Self to lead and gives you more information so you can then make an appropriate decision about what to do next.
I: Investigate.	"Thank you for talking with me, jealous part. I want to make sure I'm clear—are you jealous because you want to travel, or jealous because our friend didn't invite us on her trip?"	Investigating allows you to get clarity on the issue. If the jealous part wants to take more trips, you'll need a different intervention than if the jealous part is feeling excluded by your friend.

ALIGN Step	What It Sounds Like	What This Does
G: Give gratitude.	"Thank you for bringing this to my attention, jealous part—I really appreciate that you're here. You're important to me, and without your help, I would have no idea who I am or what I want. Grateful for you."	Extending gratitude inward allows for nervous system regulation and "thinking brain" access, and it builds internal trust.
N: Negotiate.	"Okay, I understand you want to travel more. That makes sense. It probably isn't wise to put a vacation on our credit card. But what if we start a Pinterest board with all the trip ideas that sound fun, and in the meantime, I'll plan a day trip so we can have an experience of traveling right away."	Once you've agreed to a negotiation, you'll notice the jealous part settle, allowing you to feel less fused with it and more able to choose your response. You may need to return to the negotiation table from time to time and check in to see how the part is faring.

Conclusion

Without an active Self in charge of *every* part of the inner world, humans can do awful things to one another.* Ma-

---

* Psychological experiments like the Stanford Prison Experiment and Stanley Milgram's shock experiment also showed how in the right environmental and social conditions, ordinary people can cause extraordinary harm.

rina Abramović's performance in *Rhythm 0* was a disturbing but important exposé of the dangers posed by unconscious shadows. Fortunately, the same is true on the opposite end of the spectrum. Ordinary people can also demonstrate extraordinary acts of heroism and kindness, a powerful reality illustrated by the events in the province of Newfoundland, Canada, in the aftermath of the 9/11 attacks.*

When the American airspace closed on 9/11, thirty-eight planes were diverted to a small island on the northeast edge of North America. Sixty-five hundred stranded and scared passengers descended upon Gander, a town of approximately ten thousand people. Despite the interruption to their daily lives, Newfoundlanders exhibited incredible generosity and compassion, providing food, shelter, clothing, and comfort to the "plane people." The heartwarming stories of hope, love, and human kindness amid adversity were later depicted in the Tony award-winning musical *Come from Away*. (If you haven't seen it, bring a box of tissues and be prepared to use *all* of them.)

The efforts displayed during those harrowing days were nothing short of heroic. But while *The Washington Post* dubbed Gander "The Capital of Kindness," its inhabitants are no more inherently heroic than the participants at *Rhythm 0* were innately evil. Given the right social and environmental conditions, people can show up as either the best or the worst version of themselves. When it comes to our minds, we have only two choices:

1. We can do the work to connect with our shadow parts, unleash their gifts, and welcome them home.

2. We can avoid the work of conscious connection with our shadow parts and allow them to act

---

* The Canadian provinces of Labrador, Nova Scotia, and British Columbia also participated in Operation Yellow Ribbon, which is what the diversion of civilian airline flights was called.

unconsciously. Parts may linger on the outskirts of awareness for years, decades, or an entire lifetime, but they never remain silent.

Many people fear if they venture too far inside their minds, they'll discover nothing of value. But the opposite is true. When you brave the depths of your unconscious, you're guaranteed to find buried treasure. It's one of the great joys of our Earth adventure to find out who we are and what we're capable of doing. In nature, when you look under certain rocks, it's normal to find creepy-crawly things. The same is true for your mind. I'd be more concerned by the apparent absence of hidden parts than their presence. Writer and meditation teacher Jack Kornfield beautifully articulated the human experience when he wrote:

If you can sit quietly after difficult news; if in financial downturns you remain perfectly calm; if you can see your neighbors travel to fantastic places without a twinge of jealousy; if you can happily eat whatever is put on your plate; if you can fall asleep after a day of running without a drink or a pill; if you can always find contentment just where you are:

You are probably a dog.

Bottom-Line Takeaways

1. All humans have good qualities and bad qualities.

2. Physical shadows form when light is blocked. Psychological shadows form when your awareness is blocked.

3. Shadow parts are any parts of yourself you think you shouldn't have.

4. Golden shadows are the positive qualities about yourself you either think you lack or de-emphasize because you don't want to "brag."

5. Shadow work is the process of getting honest with yourself about yourself without shaming yourself.

6. Don't do shadow work if you feel anxious or unsafe.

7. Shadows form from early childhood when aspects of yourself are unacceptable to your caregivers or culture.

8. Happiness requires wholeness, and wholeness requires connection with all your parts—including the ones you dislike or fear.

9. The three steps to shadow work are Regulate, Excavate, Activate.

10. ALIGN is an acronym you can use to connect with your parts. It stands for Acknowledge, Listen, Investigate, Give Gratitude, Negotiate.

Action Step Options

I have no time (1–5 minutes):
DECODE YOUR FEELINGS.

If you're struggling with a difficult feeling but don't have time to sit down and plumb the depths of your unconscious, use the following chart as a cheat sheet. Either think about or copy your answer into your notebook or journal:

Shadow Part	Possible Message	How might this be true for you?
Envy	There's something you authentically desire that you're not allowing yourself to admit.	
Anger	A boundary has been violated.	
Greed	You have an unmet need.	
Gossip	You feel lonely and desire authentic connection.	

I have some time (5–15 minutes):
FIND A SHADOW PART.

The five places shadow parts tend to hide include:

1. Childhood ambitions
2. People who annoy you
3. People who spark jealousy
4. Your favorite shows
5. Celebrities you admire

For each of the five places, either think about, make a list in your notebook, or journal five possible answers for each item on the list. When you have more time, choose one of your answers, name the relevant shadow part ("the one who _____"), and then use the ALIGN tool (see the next action step) to connect with that part.

I'll make time (15–45 minutes):
ALIGN with your shadow part.

Complete both the preceding tasks, then put ALIGN into action. Either think about or copy your answer into your journal or notebook.

ALIGN Step	Write your response *to* your part and/or what you hear *from* your part	What This Does
A: Acknowledge your availability.		Defuses you from your jealous part. You are not your jealousy and your jealousy is not you.
L: Listen.		Inquiry allows your Self to lead and gives you more information so you can then make an appropriate decision about what to do next.
I: Investigate.		Ask clarifying questions to make sure you fully understand your parts' feelings and the nature of the situation.

ALIGN Step	Write your response *to* your part and/or what you hear *from* your part	What This Does
G: **Give gratitude.**		Extending gratitude inward allows for nervous system regulation and access to your "thinking brain," keeping you out of the fusion states of fight, flight, freeze, or fawn. We talk a lot about the power of extending gratitude *out*. Less talked about but equally powerful is extending gratitude *in*.
N: **Negotiate.**		Negotiating a solution with your parts does the same thing as a negotiation at work. When all parties feel heard, compromises are easier to land on, and when all parties feel like they are getting some of their needs met and all their needs heard, things tend to coast more smoothly.

Part Two

Meet Your Parts

In Part Two, you'll get to know the different parts of yourself on a deeper level. We'll explore how to turn your inner critic into an ally and collaborate with your protector parts. We'll rethink the roles of compulsive behaviors and understand the needs hiding below the surface. And finally, you'll learn self-parenting techniques to nurture and guide your younger parts.

Chapter 4

Your Inner Critic Is Your Ally

How to Work with Protector Parts

When we direct a lot of hostile energy toward the inner critic, we enter into a losing battle.

—Sharon Salzberg

When life handed me lemons, I joined a cult.

Some people use drugs or alcohol to drown out the voice of the relentless inner critic. Others turn to overworking, comfort eating, or financial recklessness. Many people numb out their head noise by attaching to unavailable romantic partners. And to be clear—I tried all of those, too. Repeatedly. In the next chapter I'll share tales from my tango with addiction. But *nothing* temporarily dulled the sharp edge of my inner critic quite like cult life.

I'll explain.

While extremist cults get the lion's share of media attention, there's a wide spectrum onto which most cults fall, and it's easier than you'd think to get hooked. Why would anyone willingly subject themselves to the insanity of a cult? Cult leaders are marketing geniuses, and the allure of acceptance can be irresistible for anyone who's ever felt isolated or broken.

Imagine if Ikea had a section next to the couches and kitchens and tiny homes (yes, that's a thing) where you could purchase a prefabricated *mind*. Inside the box, you'd find an easy-to-assemble set of values, beliefs, food preferences, playlists, social customs, and language norms. Simply follow the directions and poof—you're a person. Accessories sold separately.

In my early twenties, my stormy psyche was plagued with what's commonly (and mistakenly) called borderline personality disorder,* so I was easily seduced by the idea of bypassing the trial-and-error process of cultivating an inner world. According to the friendly cult ambassadors, I didn't have to feel my feelings, think my thoughts, or have any doubts? *Sign me up*, my twentysomething self decided. So I packed up my bags and headed out on a journey that took me first to a remote town in northern California, then to a sister sect in Missouri, where I was welcomed into the fold as a beloved daughter. My inner critic's voice was temporarily (and blissfully) silenced amid the all-night prayer, multiday fasts, and rigid rituals.

Cultish author Amanda Montell nailed it when she wrote, "Modern cultish groups feel comforting in part because they help alleviate the anxious mayhem of living in a world that presents almost too many possibilities for who to be (or at least the illusion of such) . . . millennials' parents told them they could grow up to be whatever they wanted, but then that cereal aisle of endless 'what ifs' and 'could bes' turned out to be so crushing, all they wanted was a guru to tell them which to pick." The surrender to non-negotiable rules and a charismatic leader (who as of the time of writing this chapter has publicly admitted to a history of sexually predatory

---

* The symptoms of and pain caused by BPD (borderline personality disorder) are *very* real. But as you read in chapter 1, since you have multiple parts of your personality and all your parts have a job to do, there's no such thing as a personality disorder. BPD would more accurately be called complex post-traumatic stress with ambivalent attachment features.

behavior) provided relief from my incessant anxiety, hostile inner critic, and uncertainty about life.

But if you haven't guessed by now, joining a cult to silence my inner voices wasn't a great plan. What initially felt like relief quickly spiraled into childlike obedience and a dangerous dependency on the group and its leaders. But after a few years of stranger-than-fiction shenanigans, I reawakened my capacity for critical thinking and the clock on my departure began to tick.

The word *critic* often evokes negative connotations. And yes, critics can certainly be mean, judgy, and quick to rip people apart with scathing personal attacks. But I disagree with Theodore Roosevelt's declaration that "It is not the critic who counts." If you're unfamiliar with Roosevelt's "The Man in the Arena" speech, he encourages people to step up and act instead of passively observing or judging from the sidelines. The speech is inspiring, and I understand its mass appeal (and political intent). But when we interpret his words to mean "criticism is bad," we unintentionally dump constructive feedback into the proverbial trash alongside keyboard warrior wisdom and armchair expertise.

Perhaps a slight rewording is in order—it isn't *only* the critic who counts. And while, as Roosevelt said, the "doer of deeds" is the one "whose face is marred by dust and sweat and blood," without the *right* kind of criticism, we wouldn't have made it to the arena in the first place. Just ask Rocky or Daniel LaRusso.

Cynicism is anathema to growth. Constructive criticism is a requirement.

Rethinking the Inner Critic

If you've ever heard a voice in your head sneer, *You're ugly*, *You're a failure*, or *You're worthless*, you're not alone. Many (if not all) people have had the unpleasant experience of tangling with a mean voice inside their minds. The term *inner critic* first gained popularity in the 1970s courtesy of Drs. Hal and Sidra Stone, creators of *voice dialogue*.

Voice dialogue is a therapeutic technique that, like Internal Family Systems (IFS), helps people connect with and develop a more harmonious relationship with their parts. The methods and ideology of IFS and voice dialogue differ, but the guiding principle is the same—your mind is made of parts. One (or more) of those parts is prone to hurl criticism your way any time you step out of your comfort zone. You'll know this part of you is working overtime when you experience any of the following:*

1. Fear of failure

2. Perfectionism

3. Comparing yourself to others

4. Feeling inadequate

5. Impostor syndrome

6. Difficulty accepting compliments

7. Negative self-talk

8. Unrealistic expectations of yourself

9. Mistake intolerance

10. Indecisiveness

Left to its own devices, the inner critic's voice can be brutal. But when properly trained, fed, and cared for, your inner critic becomes a powerful ally, a fierce protector, and a valu-

---

* This list contains the characteristics of one cultural type of inner critic. For some cultures, the inner critic might sound like "Don't be too ambitious" or "Don't stand out."

able member of your inner team. The origin of *critic, critical,* and *criticism* comes from two Greek roots—*kriticos* (meaning discerning judgment) and *kriterion* (meaning standards). More simply put, *critical* means using your best judgment to make a decision. Criticism, when handled with compassion and skill, is a powerful growth catalyst.

In the previous chapter, you learned about shadow parts, including why connection with your shadow parts is a prerequisite for wholeness and happiness. Working with critical parts follows a similar path, but with one major difference—the level of your initial awareness. Shadow parts hide in your subconscious, and sometimes a search party is required to find them. Critical parts don't hide—they shout at the top of their lungs. Since you won't need to expend any energy looking for your inner critic, in this chapter we'll debunk the myth that your inner critic is your enemy, learn where its voice originated, and talk about practical ways to collaborate with it. Many people battle critical inner voices for their entire lives, but when you know how to align your mind, *you won't be one of them.*

The Inner Critic's Job Description

At first glance, it seems like the mean little voice in your head has one goal—to make you miserable. If a company wanted to recruit an inner critic, the posting might sound like this:

Are you looking for a dynamic role in a fast-paced work environment? If you constantly second-guess yourself, we have the perfect job for you! Currently seeking an Inner Critic to join our rapidly expanding team. Responsibilities include destroying enthusiasm and making life miserable. This role oversees the tasks of magnifying mistakes and minimizing confidence. The ideal candidate will possess a keen eye for flaws, the ability to view successes as failures, and a demonstrated knack for self-deprecation.

Educational Requirements:

Advanced training in overthinking, preferably with five years minimum experience in ruminating and perfectionism.

Salary Range:

Competitive salary commensurate with your ability to tear down every aspect of your performance. Potential for bonuses based on demonstrated commitment to self-loathing and unrealistic personal standards.

Apply within.

The problem with this job description? It's wrong on every level. Your inner critic doesn't want to destroy your life—it wants to save it.

Wait . . . what? How could that horrible inner voice want to save my life?

As you read earlier, your brain is not wired to thrive—it's wired to survive. At the first sign of danger (even if you logically think there's no reason to feel unsafe), your brain sends out the bat signal to summon survival parts. Once triggered, survival parts use stress hormones, panic, depression, fight/flight/freeze/fawn, and any other biological methods available to keep you from getting eaten by frilled-neck lizards.*

Many people (including licensed professionals) view the discomfort of survival symptoms as disorders. But discomfort does not equal disorder (squats are uncomfortable, but they're good for you), just like "feeling good" does not equal healthy

---

* The frilled-neck lizard looks like the poison-spitting dinosaur from *Jurassic Park*. Technically, the frilled-neck lizard isn't dangerous, but the name is too funny not to include.

(cocaine feels great, but it's bad for you). When we try to solve for symptoms, it's easy to forget that even highly problematic symptoms are signals. This includes messages from your inner critic. Your inner critic is not your nemesis—it's more akin to a jittery guard dog in need of love, patience, and compassion.

The Surprising Job of the Inner Critic

Many of us learned to treat our bodies and minds like they're out to get us. But the enemy of your well-being does *not* live inside you. If it did, there'd be no escape. The inner critic is a protective part whose job is to keep you safe. You may not think something should be dangerous, but just as you don't get a choice about survival responses, you don't get to decide what raises your inner critic's hackles.

Try as we may to suppress, silence, numb out, ignore, or project our parts onto other people, those parts are permanent residents of our mind, and we can't amputate them— nor would we want to once we recognize who they are and what they've done on our behalf. Many of the symptoms we learned to pathologize are the result of brains doing what brains are supposed to do—conserve energy, look for patterns, and preserve our life functions. If you were to rewrite the inner critic's job description with accurate language, it would sound more like this:

> Seeking a highly motivated candidate for a permanent position in a hostile work environment. This thankless role is responsible for safeguarding against potential threats, both real and imagined. The ideal candidate will be prepared to be misunderstood and disliked by the person they're sworn to protect. Key responsibilities include safety evaluations, risk management, and prevention of all efforts that could lead to rejection or abandonment.

The *methods* of an untrained inner critic are objectionable, but its *intentions* are always good. Your inner critic is your ally—**not** your adversary.

Origin of Your Inner Critic

The brain structure needed for self-inflicted loathing doesn't fully develop until later in life. Babies don't come into the world with an inner critic pre-installed. No infant on earth lies in their bassinet thinking, *I feel bad for crying all the time. I don't want to bother anyone to change my diaper. I can do it myself. Or maybe I'll just lie here. It's fine. I don't need anything. I should stop crying. There's no reason to cry. I'm a terrible baby.*

At birth, our mushy oatmeal brains are still forming, unable to tell the difference between ourselves and our mothers. And then it takes another year or two to discover other people have their own thoughts and feelings. But once we get the hang of toddlerhood, the inner critic's voice begins to appear. If the people around us are hard on themselves, saying things like "I can't do anything right" or "I'm such a loser," our minds soak that language up and start replaying it in our own heads.

Some researchers suggest critical self-talk emerges during preschool, while others argue that it becomes more pronounced during adolescence. Even if you had amazing parents, peers who never mocked you, and no childhood trauma, adolescence is a rough transition for even the healthiest humans. Besides the pimples, oily skin, and hormonal tornado, we're also trying to learn algebra, navigate crushes, and figure out who we are and how to human. Social pressure is off the charts. This is prime time for the inner critic to jump off the bench.

And then there's the transition out of adolescence. Launching into adulthood with an untrained inner critic is like moving into your first apartment and realizing you're stuck with a very loud roommate (with terrible taste in music). With no parents to fight with or blame, you're suddenly juggling bills, budgets, a job that expects you to know what you're doing, and relationships that feel like they require a PhD in communication to navigate. And there's your inner critic, perched on the lifeguard chair of your mind, bullhorn in hand, barking at you: *You're doing that wrong! Seriously, you thought that was a good idea?* or *Ah, so we're going with the "look what the cat dragged in" hairdo today?*

There's no exact age for the inner critic's arrival, as factors influencing its onset include your upbringing, social environment, and personal experiences. And its voice reemerges with new doubts and concerns throughout every life stage. But sadly, it's not uncommon to hear children as young as two or three say to themselves, "You're stupid." We learn to speak to ourselves with the same tone and language we hear from the humans around us. If you had parents or caregivers who criticized themselves, other people, or especially you, you'll pick up the bully ball and run with it.

Why Does This Happen?

Children criticize themselves to prevent rejection or disapproval from caregivers. For self-sufficient adults, rejection is painful, not lethal. But when infants and children are dismissed by caregivers, danger levels reach critical mass. For a helpless child, disapproval can equal death. To enhance their odds of survival, children bend themselves into any shape necessary to align with the preferences, customs, and rules of their caregivers. If their parents engage in self-critical behavior, children follow suit. Some unskilled parents instruct their kids to "do as I say, not as I do"—but that's not how humans develop. Children learn through observation. If while you were growing up, you saw your mother constantly berate herself in the mirror or heard your father say mean things to himself, those words get deposited in your bank of beliefs. The resulting internalized message is *This is what we do in this family, and if you don't do what we do, you won't be in this family for long.*

Mimicking the behaviors of caregivers helps reduce anxiety in children by providing them a sense of familiarity. Children rely on caregivers for cues on how to interpret the world around them. When caregivers demonstrate consistency—even if their behaviors are harmful—it creates a sense of stability and security. For a child (and for many adults), a predictably negative outcome is preferable to a nebulous cloud of uncertainty.

The Inner Critic and Uncertainty

Since your brain loves patterns and predictions, uncertainty throws a wrench in the wiring. The preference for consistency—even if it's negative—is a way we try to feel more in control over our lives. Uncertainty makes your brain work harder to assess threat levels and can put you in a heightened state of arousal. The inner critic is your brain's solution to this problem. If you might do something wrong, your brain is likely to prefer the certainty of failure over a potentially positive but unknown result. Self-inflicted rejection doesn't feel good, but it's an effective way to guarantee an outcome. Your inner critic gains its information and tactics from a variety of sources:

Harsh and Critical Upbringing
Negative or critical feedback from parents, caregivers, or other authority figures during your childhood contributes to the formation of your inner critic. Overly high expectations or frequent punishment can create repetitive self-talk loops. This constant barrage of negativity not only shapes a child's self-view but also sets the stage for a lifelong habit of self-

doubt and self-criticism. It can make the concept of self-compassion foreign and even uncomfortable.

Rewards and Reinforcements

If as a child, you helped your classmates with their assignments but never asked for anything yourself—not even for biological necessities like food, sleep, or bathroom breaks—you might have been labeled "a good kid." As a result of the praise heaped on you for being selfless and too giving, you may have received the message (however unintentional) that taking care of yourself is bad. This can lead to a habit of ignoring legitimate needs and feelings in adulthood, placing the well-being of others so far ahead of your own that self-neglect becomes a norm. Over time, this might evolve into a deep-seated belief that self-care is selfish, further entrenching the inner critic's hold on your psyche.

Traumatic Experiences

Traumatic experiences such as abuse and neglect have particularly dire consequences in childhood. Since the maturity (and brain structure) needed to contextualize negative experiences is absent, kids assume (unless told otherwise) bad things happen to them because they either *deserved* it or *caused* it. Traumatic experiences often reinforce negative beliefs and contribute to the development of an overly critical inner voice. This inner voice can become a relentless echo of past traumas, amplifying every mistake and setback with an undertone of self-blame and perpetuating a shame cycle that can last for years.

Peer Pressure

Peers, teachers, and other influential people contribute to the strength and power of your inner critic. Bullying, teasing, and constant comparisons to others can foster feelings of inadequacy and self-doubt, leading to a habit of negative self-talk.

This unending comparison and quest for acceptance becomes automated, causing you to critique yourself through the harshest lens possible, overlooking personal achievements and gifts and focusing on perceived shortcomings and failures.

Culture and Society

Cultural ideals, societal standards, and media representations of success and beauty contribute to our unrealistic expectations and feelings of not measuring up. These messages fuel the inner critic. Human brains were never meant to be privy to events in every corner of existence. But with screens waging a 24/7 assault on our attention, it's hard not to compare ourselves to the extraordinary beauty, wealth, and talent of people we see online. This constant bombardment creates a fertile ground for the inner critic to thrive, pushing us toward an endless pursuit of perfection that is neither achievable nor fulfilling, while we ignore the beauty of authentic, unfiltered life.

When you were a child, your inner critic was an all-star player in the game of "just survive." And if you're reading these words, congratulations—your inner critic successfully performed its duties and kept you alive. But the psychological contortion required to stay in your caregivers' good graces came with a price. Your inner critic created alignment with the people *around* you at the expense of alignment *within* you. To realign with the truth of who you are and not who you were told you should be, we'll need to first differentiate between the two types of criticism.

The Two Types of Criticism

The inner critic is like a head coach. For every Mike Krzyzewski ("Coach K") revered for integrity, self-discipline, and leadership skills, there's another group of coaches throwing chairs, punching players, and smashing hockey sticks (a quick search reveals the wildest coach meltdowns of all time). While these behaviors are utterly inexcusable, from a "survival brain" standpoint, they make sense. When a coach's brain— for whatever reason—equates losing with literal death, the fight-or-flight response ignites, resulting in viral video–worthy outbursts. Somehow this type of coach seems to forget their duties lie in the world of *sports*, not *combat*. As you read in chapter 2, brains often misinterpret nonlethal threats. Similarly, your inner critic reacts with the same primal instincts. Unless we actively do the work of questioning and recalibrating its beliefs, *survival at all costs* remains the default setting. Within this framework, the inner critic manifests itself in two distinct forms: expansion-oriented and prevention-oriented.

- The expansion-oriented inner critic is a **coach** who wants to **enhance life.**
- The prevention-oriented inner critic is a **controller** who wants to **ensure survival.**

From this point onward, we'll call the expansion-oriented inner critic "the coach" and the prevention-oriented inner critic "the controller." Using accurate terms can help you recognize and defuse from survival-based inner voices.

Expansion-Oriented Inner Critic: The Coach	Prevention-Oriented Inner Critic: The Controller
Encourages	Discourages
Pushes you forward	Holds you back
Wants you to expand	Wants you to stay small
Goal is to enhance life	Goal is to prevent death

Expansion-Oriented Inner Critic: The Coach	Prevention-Oriented Inner Critic: The Controller
Collaborative	Domineering
Bases conclusions on current information	Bases conclusions on outdated information
Generates solutions	Creates problems

The goal is not to silence the inner critic, but to transform its role from controller to coach.

A good coach toes the line between validating and challenging their team, and they recognize excessive praise can hinder development as much as if not more so than harsh criticism. And just like a healthy coach-player dynamic enhances capacity so, too, does the expansion-oriented inner critic. To turn the inner critic from a controller into a coach, we need to defuse from parts who learned to equate *approval* with *survival*. If we stay fused with survival parts, our inner critic will continue to operate on outdated information from childhood and stay stuck in the role of controller.

How can you shift your inner critic from controller to coach?

Shift your inner critic from controller to coach.

The tool that's most useful to accomplish this goal comes from the world of cognitive behavioral therapy.

What Is Cognitive Behavioral Therapy (CBT)?

CBT is an evidence-based method of talk therapy that helps people identify, understand, and challenge thoughts and change behaviors. While it has limitations (many of them),

CBT is considered the gold standard in mental health treatment and is often the first-line defense with depression and anxiety. But you don't need to suffer from a mental health condition to benefit from the tools and techniques in CBT. Frankly, I'm surprised this stuff isn't taught to adolescents alongside math and history. It should be.

CBT teaches practical strategies to manage emotions, improve problem-solving skills, and change negative thought patterns. One of the first things you'll learn in CBT is how to identify and work with cognitive distortions. Cognitive distortions (aka thinking errors) are defined as "thoughts that cause individuals to perceive reality inaccurately." I prefer to simply call them *thought patterns*. Working with thought patterns is a powerful way to transform your inner critic from controller to coach.

Rewriting Thought Patterns

Unless you were raised by perfect parents, your younger self needed their inner critic to play the role of controller. But the controller does not automatically update its belief system as you grow and learn to keep yourself alive without adult supervision. If we don't deconstruct our controller's thought patterns, its beliefs are accepted as infallible. If disapproval equaled danger *then,* it will also equal danger *now.* I've lost count of the times I've heard clients say things like this about their inner critic:

> *"I **have** to criticize myself or I won't get things done."*

> *"Yelling at myself gives me motivation."*

> *"If I don't criticize myself, I'm afraid I will get lazy."*

> *"If I don't listen to my inner critic, I'm afraid I'll lose my edge."*

"I need my inner critic to keep me humble."

"If I don't listen to my inner critic, I'll end up making mistakes and bad things will happen."

While these sentiments may have reflected the reality of your childhood, they do not match the autonomy and capability of your adult Self.* When we obey the controller (or any external leader) without question, we mimic the distorted thinking of someone stuck in a high-control group—with similar emotional and physical consequences.

It's Not All in Your Head

Even though the inner critic is a part of your mind, you live in a body. You can't separate your mind from your body. Mental health is not solely a mental process—it's also a physical process. Learning to uninstall thought patterns and challenge your controller assumptions isn't solely a mindset issue. If you're locked in a controller-critic cycle, there's a different chemical reaction in your body than when the coach is in charge. When your mind talks, your body responds. As you read in chapter 2, there are two types of stress—eustress (the good stress), which preps you to take charge, and distress (the bad stress), which inhibits and interrupts your ability to suit up and show up.

The Controller's Stress Response (Distress): When the controller is in charge, it yells at you. This can cause your brain to release stress hormones like cortisol. The release of stress hormones creates a fight/flight/freeze response in your body. This produces things like shutdown and anxiety, which make you perform poorly.

---

* Assuming the adult has sufficient safety, capacity, and access to choices.

The Coach's Stress Response (Eustress): When the coach is in charge and they encourage or challenge you, your brain releases get-up-and-go chemicals like dopamine and norepinephrine. This causes you to feel psyched and pumped and ready to go for gold.* This results in optimized performance.

Working with your inner critic is not a fluffy "let's all hold hands" exercise or a toothless directive to "just be nice to yourself." There are physical and even medical implications to our internal communication styles. When your inner critic is in coach mode, you're more likely to stay defused from survival parts, access your Self (the leader of all the parts), and land in the flow zone. The reality of the controller and coach stress responses demonstrates the profound connection between our thoughts, emotions, and physical reactions. Identifying this connection helps us to access the parts of our brain responsible for making decisions.

To do this, we need to organize and restock our mental inventory with beliefs that more accurately reflect present-day circumstances. The immortal Sherlock Holmes said, "I consider that a man's brain originally is like a little empty attic, and you have to stock it with such furniture as you choose. A fool takes in all the lumber of every sort that he comes across, so that the knowledge which might be useful to him gets crowded out, or at best is jumbled up with a lot of other things, so that he has a difficulty in laying his hands upon it."

What does this look like practically? The order of operations is this:

Step One: *Identify* the thought pattern.

Step Two: *Examine* the origins of the thought pattern.

---

* Many high-level athletes can and do achieve peak performance with controlling and even abusive coaches. But this style of leadership comes with a high psychological price.

Step Three: *Challenge* the thought pattern with updated evidence.

Step Four: *Replace* the thought pattern.

Step One:
Identify the Thought Pattern

Let's look at how some of the more common thought patterns* fuel your inner critic. You may recognize your controller's voice in some or all the following:

Nine Common Thought Patterns

THOUGHT PATTERN	DEFINITION	HOW THE PREVENTION-ORIENTED INNER CRITIC USES IT
Confirmation Bias	Looking for proof of what you already believe and ignoring evidence to the contrary.	Let's pretend you're self-conscious about being clumsy. Your controller waits until you trip and then says, *See! I told you! You're clumsy!* while ignoring all the times you walk without tripping.
All-or-Nothing Thinking	Looking at only the extreme ends of a situation without considering the middle ground.	Your controller says, *I'm warning you now. Unless you get the best review of anyone on your team, you're totally worthless.*

* Cognitive distortions were first noted by Aaron Beck in his research with depressed patients in the 1960s. They formed a central part of his cognitive theory of depression and, later, cognitive behavioral therapy.

THOUGHT PATTERN	DEFINITION	HOW THE PREVENTION-ORIENTED INNER CRITIC USES IT
Overgeneralization	Drawing broad conclusions based on limited evidence.	After receiving one rejection from a potential employer, your controller says, *You're a failure and you'll never get hired anywhere.*
Mental Filter	Focusing on the negative while ignoring the positive.	After posting a poem online, you receive dozens of positive comments and one mean comment. Your controller fixates on the one negative comment and says, *That was stupid to share your poem. Everyone hates your writing, so don't ever try to share again.*
Jumping to Conclusions	Believing something without supporting evidence.	When your friend doesn't text back immediately, your controller says, *They hate you! They're mad at you and this friendship is over!*
Personalization	Taking responsibility for things that have nothing to do with you or are outside your control.	When an unseasonably cold front sweeps in and kills your azaleas, your controller says, *It's your fault the flowers died. This is why we can't have nice things.*

THOUGHT PATTERN	DEFINITION	HOW THE PREVENTION-ORIENTED INNER CRITIC USES IT
Catastrophizing	Assuming the worst possible outcome will happen.	You're running five minutes late for a meeting, and your controller says, *You are the worst employee of all time, and they are definitely going to fire you for being late.*
Internal Control Fallacy	Feeling like there's nothing you can do about a situation when you do have choices.	Your controller says, *No matter how hard you try, you'll never succeed, because the odds are always stacked against you and there's nothing you can do.*
Labeling	Assigning overly simplistic and negative labels to yourself while ignoring the broader context.	You worked hard all week, but when you try to watch a show on Sunday, your controller says, *You're being lazy! Get up and clean the kitchen.*

Step Two:
Examine the Origins of the Thought Pattern

By acknowledging the origins of your controller's voice, you can begin to reassess threat levels. To do this, we'll use a strategy from a close cousin to CBT called rational emotive behavior therapy (REBT). CBT and REBT are similar, but while CBT puts a heavy emphasis on *behaviors*, REBT focuses more on identifying and challenging *beliefs*. If we were doing an REBT session together, we'd identify an event, assess your controller's belief about the event, then log the resulting feelings and subsequent actions. Here's an example of how it works:

Romy came to therapy to help break a pattern of chronic under-earning. They felt stuck in their job and ready to take on a bigger role, but every time a job posting showed up, their thoughts would cause body constrictions, nausea, and waves of shame that knocked them out for several days. In our first few sessions, we used REBT to help them clearly identify the problem:

EVENT	CONTROLLER'S BELIEF	RESULTING FEELINGS	RESULTING ACTION
Romy wanted to apply for a more challenging job.	Don't put yourself out there, or they'll discover you're a fraud and you'll be humiliated.	Shame and fear.	They didn't send in their application.

Once Romy identified their controller's belief about the event, we then explored where in childhood the belief originated:

CONTROLLER'S BELIEF	WHERE IT ORIGINATED
Don't put yourself out there, or they'll discover you're a fraud and you'll be humiliated.	In third grade, Romy tried out for soccer. But when they tried to kick the ball, they missed and fell. Everyone laughed, including their family.

Troubleshooting: If you don't know where it originated, you can still move on to step three.

Step Three:
Challenge the Thought Pattern
with Updated Evidence

Fighting with your controller doesn't work. Instead of asking yourself, "Is this belief true or false?" it's more helpful to ask, "On a scale of 1 to 10, *how true* is this belief *today*?" Here's how the application of this question looks in Romy's situation.

CONTROLLER'S BELIEF	WHERE IT ORIGINATED	HOW TRUE IS THIS BELIEF TODAY?
Don't put yourself out there, or they'll discover you're a fraud and you'll be humiliated.	In third grade, Romy tried out for soccer. But when they tried to kick the ball, they missed and fell. Everyone laughed, including their family.	Romy said, "I want to apply for the new job, and it's unlikely that people will laugh at me, even if I don't get the job. On a scale of 1 to 10 (1 = 0 percent true and 10 = 100 percent true), the belief that I'll be humiliated if I apply for the job is probably a 2."

Step Four:
Replace the Thought Pattern

Once Romy and I had identified the controller's belief, located its origin, and assessed its present-day accuracy, we went back to the original chart to replace the outdated controller's belief.

EVENT	COACH'S BELIEF	RESULTING FEELINGS	RESULTING ACTION
Romy wanted to apply for a more challenging job.	It would really be a bummer to get rejected, but if you try and fail, nothing bad will happen and we can try again next year.	Excited and nervous.	Romy eventually was able to send in the application.

Disclaimer: Doing an REBT exercise (even if you have amazing pens and a beautifully crafted chart) will *not* magically transform your inner critic from controller to coach. Replacing entrenched thought patterns with new beliefs is a bit like receiving an organ transplant. It can take time for the new belief to integrate with your system, and sometimes your mind may initially reject the coach's beliefs. This is totally normal. If it was easy to simply replace thinking patterns and call it a day, no one would need therapy and there wouldn't be a bajillion books on the subject. This process takes practice, so if you're having trouble with your inner critic, *please* don't criticize yourself. Criticizing yourself for how you do your inner critic work is some serious meta-criticism.

Instead, use the chart as a starting place to help dial down your system's reactivity. Once you bring yourself from a level 10 to a 5 or 6, you can move on to the following three strategies.

From Controller to Coach: Three Strategies

Strategy One:
Affirm Your Inner Critic by Saying, "Yeah, That's Probably a Little Bit True"

Honoring the kernel of truth in any accusation helps to decrease its sting. And since you are a complex being with infinite parts, when you hear your inner critic lob *any* accusation, no matter how illogical, you can affirm to yourself, "Yeah, that's probably a little bit true." Allowing for nuance helps prevent binary thinking.

Strategy Two:
Use Your Body to Confuse Your Brain

Sometimes there is no amount of thought work, journaling, or even meditating that can help out-of-control thoughts. When this happens—and it happens to *all* of us (as I was writing this chapter my own controller's voice made a cameo)—it helps to get out of your head by moving your body. And "moving your body" *doesn't* refer to burning calories or working out. The purpose of this strategy is to move in such a way that your brain gets confused. Hop backward on your nondominant foot. Try rubbing your head and patting your stomach while walking in a circle. Dance fast to slow music, or dance slow to fast music. This sounds strange, but any time you snow-globe your brain, it's easier to switch out of autopilot mode.

Strategy Three:
DEFUSE

You'll see this acronym throughout this book, and you can use it any time you feel fused with your inner critic and unable to get yourself out of a mind loop. Refer to chapter 2 for a more detailed explanation:

D: Describe your physical sensations.
   (either out loud or in your notebook or journal)

E: Exit the room.

F: Feel your body.

U: Use your senses.

S: Shift.

E: Exhale.

Conclusion

Examining thought patterns and learning to reinstall a more constructive inner voice is a lifelong process. Just like any long-term relationship, you're never done with your critic (or any of your parts). As you continue to practice this work, you'll discover an untapped well of resiliency, capacity, and drive. If you want to get unstuck and move past what holds you back, you *don't* need to conform to social media standards or align with the people around you. My detour into a cult group was an extreme example, but the temptation to flee from our thoughts is universal. Following somebody else's handbook reduces uncertainty but obliterates authenticity. A Self-led life, no matter how messy, is usually preferable to someone else's "just add water and stir" solution.

So when life hurls lemons, limes, or any other type of citrus your way, remember your inner critic is your ally, and it wants to help you get wherever you want to go. In the end, I came to discover collaborating with the inner critic is preferable to the unquestioning obedience and conformity required to silence its voice. Whether it's the latest wellness fad, fitness obsession, or get-rich-quick pyramid scheme, I encourage you to think twice before jumping on board anything that sounds like this:

Hey there! I've come across this amazing opportunity that's changed my life and can totally change yours! Want to learn more?

Bottom-Line Takeaways

1. Not all criticism is bad.

2. Your inner critic's role is not destructive, but protective.

3. Inner critic beliefs largely stem from childhood experiences.

4. We learn to criticize ourselves as children to prevent disapproval or rejection.

5. The inner critic helps reduce uncertainty.

6. The expansion-oriented inner critic wants you to thrive.

7. The prevention-oriented inner critic wants you to survive.

8. Identifying thought patterns is the first step to shifting from prevention to expansion.

9. Assessing and replacing outdated thought patterns is the second step.

10. Cults are not a sustainable way to silence your inner voices.

Action Step Options

I have no time (1–5 minutes).

If you're super short on time, you don't have to fight with your inner critic or do the work of deconstructing its thought patterns. Instead, simply extend it the same compassion and understanding you would a child who is trying to help in the kitchen but making a huge mess. You can say this to the critical part of you:

"I understand you are trying to help me. Thank you for being part of my inner team. I will do my best to keep us alive so you don't have to work so hard."

I have some time (5–15 minutes).

Challenge your thought patterns. Take a few minutes and either think about or write in your notebook or journal your answers to the following:

- What is the belief of my inner critic?
- Where did it learn this?
- What is the current truth?
- What would a supportive coach say instead?

I'll make time (15–45 minutes).

Do the other two exercises and then ALIGN with your inner critic.

ALIGN Step	Write your response *to* your inner critic and/or what you hear *from* your inner critic.	What This Does
A: Acknowledge your availability.		Defuses you from your critical parts. You are not your critic, and your critic is not you.

ALIGN Step	Write your response *to* your inner critic and/or what you hear *from* your inner critic.	What This Does
L: Listen.		Inquiry allows your Self to lead and gives you more information so you can then make an appropriate decision about what to do next.
I: Investigate.		Ask clarifying questions to make sure you fully understand your parts' feelings and the nature of the situation.
G: Give gratitude.		Extending gratitude inward allows for nervous system regulation and access to your "thinking brain," and keeps you out of the fusion states of fight, flight, freeze, or fawn. We talk a lot about the power of extending gratitude *out*. Less talked about but equally powerful is extending gratitude *in*.
N: Negotiate.		Negotiating a solution with your parts does the same thing as a negotiation at work. When all parties feel heard, compromises are easier to land on, and when all parties feel like they are getting some of their needs met and all their needs heard, things tend to coast more smoothly.

Chapter 5

Can't Stop, Won't Stop

Rethinking Compulsive Parts

The trick to overcoming addiction is thus the realignment of desire, so that it switches from the goal of immediate relief to the goal of long-term fulfillment.

—Dr. Marc Lewis, *The Biology of Desire: Why Addiction Is Not a Disease*

I staggered with uncertainty, barely managing one shaky step before I collapsed. With my face pressed against the cold floor, I felt a drip of blood trickling onto my hands as the sharp burn of my scraped-up legs seared through me. Amid the dizzying sensations in my head, I fought back the urge to empty my stomach, focusing instead on drawing in ragged breaths. This wasn't the first time I'd found myself in this position, nor would it be the last.

But it isn't what you think.

The dramatics described above weren't the aftermath of a drug bender, nor the result of a harrowing domestic dispute (not this time, at least). My wobbly state and blurry vision weren't alcohol induced or due to sleep deprivation—I was completely sober and wide-awake. So what was going on? This scene was all thanks to a circus rehearsal, where I had unsuccessfully attempted to complete a three-minute aerial hoop routine.

Let me back up and explain.

Any time the circus is in town, I find a way to go see it. But I always thought aerial arts were reserved for ethereal beings masquerading as mortals—not an activity for regular humans. And certainly not for *this* human, who took her sweet time giving up a two-decade-long habit of smoking a pack of Marlboros a day (which clocks in at more than 100,000 cigarettes, if you're counting—yikes). Nevertheless, I found myself hypnotized by possibility while attending an amateur circus performance. The people onstage weren't lifelong pros—these were accountants and nurses and real estate agents. I sat in the dark, spellbound, as a beautiful woman on a spinning metal hoop gracefully descended from the ceiling. Fueled by the fire of my personal life burning to the ground, I made a split-second decision: *I am going to become an aerialist.* And if that wasn't delusional enough, I also told myself, "Someday I'm going to perform a solo in this theater."

I was thirty-six. Not exactly a spring chicken.

Before my doubtful inner voices could scrap the idea, I found an aerial hoop coach and began training. It was *awful. Awkward* doesn't even begin to describe my early efforts. It took months before I could even pull myself up on the stupid thing without help. I'm directionally challenged on the ground, but once I'm airborne, my brain immediately protests and says, "Nope. Not braining today." It was so bad my coach, the talented (and exceedingly patient) Elena Sherman, would often tape different-colored Xs on my feet so I could tell my left from my right when I was upside down and spatially disoriented. I often left the gym in tears. But as *The Phantom Tollbooth* author Norton Juster put it, "So many things are possible just as long as you don't know they're impossible."

After several years of relentless effort (or stubborn naivete), I cobbled together enough skills to participate in recitals (alongside the little kids and a handful of nervous adults). Eventually I auditioned for and got accepted into a student company. After performing in the ensemble for several seasons, I qualified for solo tryouts. After nearly a year working on my audition piece, fighting to hit demanding physical requirements (like climbing a rope to the ceiling and dead-hanging off a trapeze), the audition came—and I got the part. This was happening. I was going to perform a solo in front of a paying audience—and the show was being held in the *very same theater* I'd sat in years earlier. Game on.

This brings us back to our current situation with me face-planted on the studio floor.

Once the room stopped spinning, I meekly grabbed my stuff and went home, spending the rest of the afternoon splayed on the couch, frozen vegetables strategically placed on my face, hands, and knees. Circus is a glorious blend of beauty and brutality. Scrapes, bruises, aching muscles I didn't know existed—all part of the process. Often during rehearsals, waves of nausea would knock me off my feet or my callused hands would rip open, and then it was game over for the day. Despite our minds' determination, sometimes our bodies have other plans.

Why would any sane person willingly enter an arena of such emotional and physical vulnerability? I wasn't aiming to be a professional circus performer, and it's not like I came from a family of acrobats where grace and fearlessness seem embedded in the genetic code. (I was raised by a family whose genetic makeup skewed more toward neurotic anxiety than hamstring flexibility.) Why push through the pain, terror, and nausea? Why continue to suit up and show up week after week? The answer is simple: *desire*.

My desire to participate in the beauty of circus is stronger than my desire to avoid the pain of circus. As my company director (whom I still suspect is an ethereal being hiding in a human body), Kelsey Aicher, told me, "Our apparatuses literally bruise us. We leave rehearsals crying more often than we would like to admit. We spend hundreds of hours of literal and figurative pain to have five minutes onstage. But those five minutes hold five months' worth of elation, adrenaline, and validation. We are creating art."

What Does All of This Have to Do with You?

Desire is a tricky beast. Properly harnessed, it propels us toward our passions and goals, but it's also a wrecking ball. We've all felt it in some form—the desire for an unavailable person, the craving for a third glass of wine, or the compulsion to watch just *one more* episode of *Brooklyn Nine-Nine*. Unchecked desire quickly turns destructive and even addictive. I've danced with addiction in various forms—food, substances, and people. I've tried (and failed) many times to wriggle out of its choke hold. Even if you don't identify as an "addict," *everyone* experiences problematic desires to a degree. (If you disagree, try turning off all your screens during a hectic day and see how long it takes your body to get twitchy.) Addiction is less a binary "you have it or you don't" designation and more a spectrum onto which all of us fall.

Is desire the sole force driving addiction? No. There are numerous contributing factors, including environment, family systems, genetics, access to resources, brain chemistry, and social supports. And admittedly, a single chapter in a single book (let alone a coliseum full of books) could never fully cover the complexity of addiction. The academic world continues to argue about the nature of addiction. Some experts insist addiction is a disease; others claim it's a learned behavior. Some view addiction as a morality issue and others as a problem of dopamine deficiency. There are merits to and problems with most addiction models, and this book makes no effort to validate or refute any of them. Instead, we'll examine habits from the *parts perspective,* which views addiction as an **effective but destructive way protector parts cope with pain.**

When you learn to collaborate with protector parts, you can get unstuck from even long-standing behaviors and patterns. By the end of this chapter, you won't unlock a magical portal to a habit-free existence, but you will unravel the mystery of what I call the *shame bind*—the strange scenario inside your mind where one part feels intense shame for their behavior and another part insists the behavior continue. You'll also get an answer to the age-old "Why do I keep doing this to myself?" question, along with practical strategies.

A caveat: The origins of problematic behavior can vary, and not all habits stem from unexamined wounds. If you want to skip the guided tour and head straight to the gift shop, check out chapter 9, "No Motivation Required," where I share my ultimate "change your life" tool called *micro-yeses*, which works with everything from revenge bedtime procrastination to getting fit to fixing your finances.

For everyone else, let's continue.

Rethinking Addiction

Addiction is often defined by the clinical world as a compulsive desire to repeat behaviors despite negative consequences. But this definition is simplistic and ignores a key truth about human brains—they're wired for survival. Why would a survival-oriented brain desire to repeat harmful behaviors? Many people answer that question with self-blaming explanations like:

- I must be broken.
- I must be crazy.*
- I must have an addicted personality.

---

* *Crazy* is a pejorative used to label and stigmatize behaviors we don't understand. But it's not a biological reality. There's no such thing as a crazy person.

- I want to stop, but I can't.
- I *want* to want to stop, but I'm not going to, so this must just be who I am.

Doing the same things over and over and expecting different results is *not* a sign of insanity—it's a sign of pain. Not all behavior is acceptable, but even unhealthy behaviors are functional. When we focus on *changing* behavior without *understanding* behavior, we're likely to get stuck.

Addiction is what happens when our desire to avoid pain outweighs our capacity to endure it.

More simply put? Addiction is not self-sabotage; it's self-protection. And unless we actively work to change the default settings, the impulse to self-protect stays greater than the desire to self-actualize. And because it's both relevant and true, I'll say the thing therapists aren't supposed to say: Before they destroy your body and your life, drugs are fun and they make you feel good.*

If we created a task list for your brain, the desire to avoid pain has a higher evolutionary priority than the desire to build health. There's well-documented principle called *loss aversion* at play here. Loss aversion is the tendency to feel the *pain of loss* more intensely than the *pleasure of equivalent gain*. In other words, the frustration of losing five dollars would impact you more than the joy of finding five dollars. As long as our desire for relief outweighs everything else, we'll stay stuck.

Some people think addiction is the result of an out-of-control pursuit of hedonic pleasure, but as anyone who's ever experienced its claws will attest (me included), the reality is quite the opposite. Author Edgar Allan Poe wrote:

---

* The feel-good reality of drugs is something they forgot to teach us during the 1980s D.A.R.E. programs.

I have absolutely no pleasure in the stimulants in which I sometimes so madly indulge. It has not been in the pursuit of pleasure that I have periled life and reputation and reason. It has been the desperate attempt to escape from torturing memories, from a sense of insupportable loneliness and a dread of some strange impending doom.

Your life may not be as bleak as Poe's, but most people know the feeling of repeating bad habits despite an earnest desire to stop.

Why do we do this to ourselves?

Sometimes addictions persist not because of a character defect or weakness, but because in the absence of access to resources and appropriately trained providers, there's not enough structural support to endure the pain required by the recovery process. This isn't a personal failing or character flaw—it's simply how brains function. It's not a moral issue if you get an infection in an unsterile operating room, and it's not a plant's fault if it fails to thrive in a pot full of rotted soil. Sometimes what the mental health world calls disorders or diseases are the result of systemic failures—not personal ones.

Assuming you have relative safety and access to basic needs, we'll use parts work to answer the "Why do I do things that are bad for me?" question. Fortunately, your mind already contains everything you need to begin the change process. But as Dr. Marc Lewis wrote in the epigraph to this chapter, the task is *not* to change who you are. At your core, your Self (capital S) already exists in a perfect state. Rather than changing essence, the task is to change *alignment* and switch the goal from immediate relief to long-term fulfillment.

How?

To kick-start this process, we need to look at the different parts of your mind involved with self-protection.

Your Internal Bodyguards

You read in the previous chapter how your inner critic, rather than being your enemy, is an ally who wants to keep you safe (albeit through unpleasant means). Your inner critic is part of a team of protective parts—this group is focused on *prevention*. But you also have another category of protective parts who show up when prevention efforts fail. This team arrives on the scene when your brain thinks you need immediate help.

To best understand your protector parts, we'll use the United States Secret Service as an example.* Within the Secret Service, thousands of officers, special agents, and personnel are split into four divisions—the White House Branch, Foreign Missions Branch, Vice President Residence, and the Special Operations Branch. The Secret Service calls protected individuals *principals*. During an "attack on the principal" (AOP), service members swiftly respond to the threat, neutralize it, protect the principal from harm, and deploy any means necessary to ensure the principal's ongoing safety. Your mind is structured the same way, except instead of four protective divisions, you have two: the *proactive branch* and the *reactive branch*.

PROACTIVE BRANCH	REACTIVE BRANCH
Tries to prevent pain	Tries to manage pain
Shows up in your thoughts	Shows up in your behaviors
Future focused ("Something bad might happen.")	Present focused ("Something bad is happening.")
Strategic	Spontaneous
Seeks external approval	Seeks internal relief

* Random but fun trivia: The Secret Service was established in 1865 as a bureau in the Treasury Department to suppress widespread counterfeiting.

The proactive branch includes your inner critic and other parts who nag, scold, bully, and yell at you to keep you out of trouble. The other branch is staffed by reactive protectors,* who spring into action when you feel triggered or uncomfortable. The reactive protectors employ a wide range of soothing strategies from benign late-night scrolling and morning naps to more insidious drug habits.

When Helpers Cause Harm

Many of us are well acquainted with our reactive protectors, but we learned to view them as mortal enemies instead of well-intentioned bodyguards. Reactive protectors can show up as:†

- Depression
- Hopelessness
- Rage
- Addiction
- Self-harm
- Numbing behaviors
- Self-soothing

A Part Can Be Both Protective and Harmful

Imagine a parent who sees their child about to run into on-coming traffic. Panicked, the parent yells, grabs the child by the arm, and roughly yanks them out of the way, causing a bruised and dislocated shoulder. But despite the injury, the

---

* In the Internal Family Systems model, the proactive protectors are called *Managers* and the reactive protectors are called *Firefighters*. Managers and Firefighters are tasked to protect *Exiles*, parts who carry burdens and pain from the past.

† The parts perspective doesn't discount the medical and environmental components potentially driving behaviors. Parts work is a framework that views symptoms through the lens of functionality rather than psychopathology.

parent managed to protect the kid from getting hit by a car. Mission accomplished.

Protective parts don't care about your quality of life, happiness, or mobility—they care about doing their one and only job. In the critically panned but enduring nineties classic *The Bodyguard*, Kevin Costner plays the titular character, an ex–Secret Service agent tasked to protect a superstar named Rachel (played by Whitney Houston). As she wanders through a store, their brief interaction perfectly illustrates the nature of protective parts:

Rachel: *Will you grab that jacket for me? The red one, please?*

Frank: *I'm here to keep you alive, not help you shop.*

The difference between our internal protective systems and the Secret Service is the nature of the principals. In the external world, it's only powerful celebrities and heads of state who get bodyguards. But internally, the protectees are the least powerful members of your inner society—including your younger and smaller parts, sometimes referred to as your inner child. We'll talk about inner children (you have more than one) in the next chapter.

Two Teams, One Goal

When most people think of competing inner voices, they describe images like a boxing ring or battle scene. If we were to sketch out the dominant view of habits and addictions, it would look something like this:

$$\longleftarrow \qquad\qquad\qquad\qquad \longrightarrow$$

Parts who desire good things   vs.   Parts who desire bad things

But from the parts work lens, this image is inaccurate. It *feels* like you're being pulled in two opposing directions, but destructive habits are *not* akin to a cartoon devil on your left shoulder with a harp-wielding angel on the right. Looking at addiction from the viewpoint of "sobriety good, drugs bad" isn't wrong, but it's too simplistic to solve the problem. (This is one major reason why there are such abysmal recovery rates for traditional drug treatment programs.)

Okay, so if my good parts aren't fighting my bad parts, what's going on?

People can (and do) display bad behaviors, but there's no such thing as a bad part.* If we drew an organizational chart to represent your protective system, it would look less like a tug-of-war and more like this:

There's no such thing as a bad part.

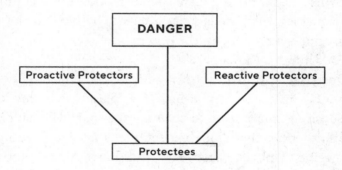

You'll notice both teams of protectors are singularly focused on their protectees. There is no line connecting the protective teams to each other. Both teams have different missions, different objectives, and different strategies, but their goal is the same—defend the principal from either real or perceived danger. Here's where things get dicey:

---

* Explanation is not synonymous with excuse. "I did a bad thing only because my parts were protecting me" may explain a behavior, but it never excuses it. "My parts made me do it" is never a valid reason for abuse.

Most of us are keenly aware of our opposing inner voices. Whenever you feel like part of you wants to go home and prep a meal and another part wants to stop for fast food, you've experienced *parts awareness*. But here's the major curveball with parts work: *even when we're aware of our parts, parts are not always aware of each other.* And when they *do* start poking and biting each other, it's because they don't know they play for the same team—*you.*

Parts work views habits and addictions less as *Clash of the Titans* and more like two departments in a company with seemingly incompatible objectives—say, accounting wants to cut the budget and marketing wants more money for ads. The problem is not between the two teams. Even though it *looks* like they're fighting each other, both have the same goal—to generate revenue and help the company succeed. But when the marketing team spends money, the accounting team may angrily demand more cuts. The behavior of one team ignites a reaction in the other.

Your mind is the same.

One part of your mind can activate the concerns of another. For instance, if you have one part who wants kids, that desire is guaranteed to elicit another part who isn't sure if parenthood is the right choice. Or let's say you have a part who wants to move to a new city; this desire triggers another part with major concerns about such a big life change. Internal Family Systems calls this dilemma *polarization*; we all experience it to varying degrees.* In their efforts to get needs met, proactive protectors polarize with reactive protectors, creating psychological tension. Any time you align with one side and reject the other, tension builds. When this happens, the unchosen side grows in strength and power until it's hard to recognize they're on your team at all.

---

* Parts polarization is *not* a claim that everyone has bipolar disorder. Nor should any of this information be taken as a sign to go off your medication. Always discuss medication and treatment with your doctor.

Whose Side Are You On?

We're often quick to align with proactive protectors, since qualities like perfectionism and people-pleasing are more socially acceptable than addiction and emotional outbursts. But all your parts have valuable messages to share with you. Trying to suppress or ignore these messages tends to make things worse. As Dr. Schwartz put it in *No Bad Parts*, "When you refuse to listen, you can turn your parts into inner terrorists, and they will destroy your body if necessary." If you've ever said something like "I hate the part of myself who procrastinates," you've rejected your procrastinator and aligned with the part of yourself who *doesn't* procrastinate. Sometimes you can white-knuckle your way through a polarization, but the more you fight your protectors, the stronger they get.

A quote often attributed to Carl Jung says it best: "What you resist, persists." And as anyone who's ever thrown shade* at their parts (and we've all done it) knows, choosing sides doesn't usually fare well. Think of a sibling squabble—if a parent sides with one of the children, the other is likely to either blow up or implode. In a perfect world, parents compassionately listen to all concerns and then decide what would best serve the whole. Working with polarized parts requires the same skill set. Rather than aligning with one side of the polarity, Jung says we need to "hold the tension of the opposites . . . this is possible only if we remain conscious of both at once."

From the parts work lens, you can begin to "hold the tension of the opposites" by reminding yourself of three things:

Trying to suppress or ignore these messages tends to make things worse.

---

* Fun fact—Merriam-Webster's first recorded use of *shade* as an insult is from the 1990 documentary *Paris Is Burning*, which chronicles the drag scene in mid-1980s Manhattan as seen through the eyes of young Latino and Black drag queens.

1. Your parts are on your side.

2. All your parts are valuable citizens of your mind.

3. The task of this work is to align your mind, not to eliminate its parts.

Even when you're conscious of both sides of a polarity, it can feel challenging to hold the tension of opposites. Jungian analyst and feminist icon Marion Woodman wrote, "Holding an inner conflict quietly instead of attempting to resolve it quickly is a difficult idea to entertain. It is even more challenging to experience . . . a hasty move to resolve tension can abort growth of the new. If we can hold conflict in psychic utero long enough, we can give birth to something new in ourselves."

More simply put? When we view habits and addictions not as problems to be solved, but as polarities to be managed, the entire game changes.

Important Disclaimer: In life-threatening crises such as an opiate overdose, the first order of business is medical stability, not psychological inquiry. There is no "holding the tension of opposite" in these types of situations. There are many instances when a medical intervention is necessary before any psychological interventions are appropriate, safe, or helpful.

When Balance Backfires

Contrary to popular opinion, the solution to polarization is *not* balance. Even a seemingly balanced solution like "When I'm done with my to-do list, I'll let myself relax" is a recipe for tension and misalignment.

How?

There are three main problems with any negotiation that

sounds like "When I do A [the good thing], then I can have B [the fun thing]":

1. By putting emphasis on doing A first, you tell your B team they're less valuable.

2. This solution fails to consider context. There are times when the fun thing (especially if it's rest) is more important than being productive.

3. Negotiating at the *level* of behavior fails to recognize the *function* of the behavior.

Instead of seeking balance, polarities are best managed with curiosity, collaboration, and a nonpartisan solution. Jung calls this the third path.

Walking the Third Path

The third path is the idea of *transcending* opposites rather than trying to find a balance between them. It's about extending curiosity toward opposing parts, rather than bouncing back and forth between them. The third path is a creative solution that allows for change while also honoring the intentions of your parts. *Third path thinking* sounds esoteric, but it's super practical. The easiest way to understand third path thinking is to look at the world of business negotiations.

High-level negotiators are likely familiar with the work of Roger Fisher. As a Harvard law professor, director of the Harvard Negotiation Project, and coauthor of the influential 1980s book *Getting to Yes*, Fisher is a giant in the business world. His concept of "position versus interest" beautifully translates to parts management. Here's how it works:

Position: In a negotiation, a *position* refers to a specific demand or stance taken by one party. With a polarization, one part's position might be *I want to spend the day drinking,* and another part's position might be *I want to spend the day cleaning.*

Interest: *Interests* are the underlying needs, concerns, or desires that drive someone's position. Positions are *what* someone wants, while interests are the why behind the want.

Let's go back to the preceding example. If you asked your drinking part why it wants a bottomless mimosa palooza, it might say, *It's been a difficult week. We'll feel better if we just let loose and relax.* If you sat down with your cleaning part and asked the same question, it might say, *It's been a difficult week. We'll feel better with a clean house.*

In this situation, your parts have the same interests. But as long as each part feels threatened by the other's position, you will continue to spin and stay stuck. Fisher wrote, "Negotiations are not likely to make much progress as long as one side believes that the fulfillment of their basic human needs is being threatened by the other." With habits and addictions, third path thinking focuses on the *interests* of the parts rather than on judging their *positions.*

This can feel counterintuitive.

Whether you struggle with an out-of-control addiction or a pesky habit, the thought of focusing on mutual inner interests seems strange. And to be clear, sometimes people *first* need a medically supervised detox and professional help (not to mention environmental stability, safety, and a non-soggy brain) before parts work is safe or useful. And even though the interests of your parts may be protective, good intentions *never* excuse bad behaviors, nor does it mean there should be no consequences for harmful actions. With parts work, you never have to accept, forgive, or enable the behaviors of someone *else's* protective parts; your job is to extend compassion toward *yours.* We'll talk more about navigating relationships in chapter 7.

To uncover the interests of your parts, instead of saying to yourself, "What's wrong with me?" ask, "What's *right* about this behavior?" As author Alan Watts put it, "Problems that remain persistently insoluble should always be suspected as questions asked the wrong way."

The Pain Problem

Both branches of your protective system want to protect you and will go to great lengths to do so—even if their efforts cause collateral damage. They will black you out, lock you down, chain you to the wall, and go to any length—sometimes even lethal—if that's what it takes to keep you away from whatever they perceive to be most threatening. As addiction expert and author Dr. Gabor Maté put it, "Ask not why the addiction, ask why the pain." Parts work views addiction and bad habits not as character defects but as pain management solutions.

"But," you ask, "what is the pain my system is trying to protect me from? Everything is fine. I had a great childhood, and nothing bad ever happened to me." You may not think you should have a pain problem, but as you read in chapter 2, your brain's safety team has access to more information than your logical mind. Not everyone needs therapy or an exhaustive exploration of their past, and parts work does *not* require you to recover repressed abuse memories or to get angry with your parents. But a discussion about habits and addictions is incomplete without bringing up the issue of pain, and talking about pain is impossible without a brief overview of trauma—a term often misunderstood (and the subject of countless debates). I wrote more extensively about trauma in *The Science of Stuck,* but we'll do a quick recap here:

What Is Trauma?

Trauma, most simply put, is *brain indigestion.* Just as eating too quickly can hinder your stomach's ability to digest food, witnessing or experiencing *any* event can strain your brain's capacity to process it. Consequently, these undigested emotions and body sensations linger in your nervous system and cause your safety team to get stuck in fight/flight/freeze/fawn responses. *Anything* has the potential to cause trauma, though not everything will.

Trauma, most simply put, is *brain indigestion.*

Is All Trauma the Same?

No. Trauma is not all the same, just as not all injuries are the same. The word *injury* can mean a scraped knee or a bullet wound. Similarly, the word *trauma* can refer to being socially rejected or to surviving an earthquake. There are certainly things we can all agree count as traumatic, such as war, poverty, assault, abuse, or systemic oppression. But there's a difference between an externally traumatic *event,* the internal process of trauma, trauma-inducing events, and trauma responses.

TERM	DEFINITION
Traumatic event	Things we can all agree are universally horrific, such as rape, assault, oppression, systemic racism, and natural disasters. Traumatic events are always bad, but they do not always cause PTSD or chronic mental health symptoms.
Trauma	An internal process in which your brain is unable to digest information and your system gets stuck in one (or several) of the four survival responses.

TERM	DEFINITION
Trauma-inducing event	Trauma-inducing events are not always bad, but they can still be overwhelming and create problems. Trauma-inducing events can include getting married, having a baby, getting a promotion, having dental work done, or moving to a new city.
Trauma response	Our external expression of internal trauma. Trauma responses can look like panic, depression, anxiety, or any other type of psychological or medical symptom.

Not all traumatic events will cause trauma responses, but sometimes mild events will. Why? Our brain's ability to digest events is based on many factors, including current resources, community support, safety, genetics, and family of origin. Unfortunately, *trauma* has become the current buzzword used for everything from "I don't like the way you chew" to "I'm trying to cope with abuse." But rather than insisting that the term be used properly or debating what should qualify as trauma, in this book we'll shift the conversation from *trauma* to *pain*. Your protector parts react to many kinds of pain. Here are my top seven:

1. **Systemic:** Lack of access to care, systemic oppression, racism, war

2. **Emotional:** Loneliness, depression, anxiety, fear, grief

3. **Existential:** Spiritual crisis, lack of meaning or purpose, fear of death, feeling disconnected from the world, feeling "floaty" or lost

4. **Relational:** Betrayal, abuse, conflict with friends, partners, family

5. **Financial**: Financial instability, debt, under-earning, unable to access needs and wants

6. **Occupational**: Burnout, overwhelm at work, abusive boss or coworkers, too many demands and not enough time

7. **Physical**: Injury, illness, medical crisis, disease, withdrawal

To help your parts better cope with pain, you'll need to replace judgment with curiosity. As Jungian analyst Robert A. Johnson put it, "One must be willing to say: 'Who are you? What do you have to say? I will listen to you. . . .' This requires a formidable realignment of attitude for most of us. If there is something in yourself you see as a weakness, a defect, a terrible obstruction to a productive life, you nevertheless have to stop approaching that part of yourself as 'the bad guy.'"

How?

When your fingers get stuck in a Chinese finger trap, you can't escape by pulling your fingers apart; the oppositional force tightens the trap. Instead, the solution is to push your fingers *toward* each other. As they get closer, space opens for you to maneuver out. The same is true for polarized parts—even with severe addiction and bad habits.

How to ALIGN with Polarized Parts

You've used the ALIGN acronym to connect with shadow parts and critical parts. Now we'll modify it slightly so you can use it with parts who struggle with habits or addictions. The difference here is instead of using the ALIGN tool with one part, you'll use it twice—once with each side of the po-larization. There are five steps to this process:

Step 1: ALIGN with your "problem" part.

Step 2: ALIGN with your "idealized" part.

Step 3: Identify mutual interests.

Step 4: List your choices.

Step 5: Negotiate a solution.

To best illustrate these steps, we'll use problematic drinking as an example. You can do the steps in your head or out loud, but it's better to write it down. There's a blank chart at the end of this chapter you can use or copy into your notebook or journal.

Step 1. ALIGN with Your "Problem" Part

A. Acknowledge.	Validate the intentions of the drinking part. Say, "I recognize you are trying to help me by drinking. I know you want to protect me from pain."
L. Listen.	Ask the part to tell you what it's afraid will happen if you don't drink. What feelings might come up? What decisions might you be faced with? Make a list of all the things you hear your drinking part share. These might include the fear of detox and withdrawal, the fear of losing a social circle, the fear of feeling lonely without alcohol, or a fear of embarrassment.
I. Identify the interests.	Once you listen to the part, you'll have a better idea of the interests (the why behind the behavior). Write down the interests separately so you can refer to them later.

| G.
Give gratitude. | Thank the part for trying to help protect you. |
| N.
Name the other part. | Let this part know about its counterpart. You can say, "There's another part here who really wants to stop drinking. You both have the same goal, and I'm not taking anyone's side." |

Step 2. ALIGN with Your "Idealized" Part

A. Acknowledge.	Validate the intentions of the nondrinking part. Say, "I recognize you are trying to help me by not drinking. I know you want to protect me from pain."
L. Listen.	Ask the part to tell you what it's afraid will happen if you drink. Make a list of all the things you hear. These might include the fear of financial and social loss or the fear of medical consequences.
I. Identify the interests.	Once you listen to the part, you'll have a better idea of the interests (the why behind the behavior). Write down the interests separately so you can refer to them later.
G. Give gratitude.	Thank the part for trying to help protect you.
N. Name the other part.	Let this part know about its counterpart. You can say, "There's another part here who thinks drinking will help solve the problem. But you both have the same goal, and I'm not taking anyone's side."

Step 3. Identify Mutual Interests

You'll notice that the interests of the drinking part and the nondrinking part may be similar or even identical. Both want to protect you. Say to your parts (or write down in your notebook or journal), "You both want the same thing. We are all on the same team, and I'm here to find the best solution for *all* of us."

Step 4: List Your Choices

Sometimes we get so bogged down in the "What do I do?" question that we forget to stop and first do the work of identifying your choices. For this step, make a list of every person, place, or thing available to help you. You don't have to like all your choices, nor do you have to make any decisions—this step is simply a list of possibilities. For the fictional drinking example, choices to address the pain problem might include going to a twelve-step meeting, going to an inpatient alcohol treatment center, calling a friend, finding outpatient substance abuse treatment, participating in an online support group, asking for help, or researching trauma therapists.

Step 5: Negotiate a Solution

Remember, solutions are not solely about behavior modification; they also need to focus on interests. For the drinking example, one of the fears of the drinker part might be isolation. (This might be especially true if your friends are also heavy drinkers.) While the ideal solution to a drinking problem might be abstinence and treatment, those choices might not be available or make sense as a starting point. Instead, a negotiation might sound like: "We are going to start by doing online research to find a group. Online support feels safer, since no one knows us and we can stay home. Then after we do a few online meetings, we'll come back to the negotiating table and make another decision."

When solutions are based on interests, you separate your *parts* from the *problem*. And when you see your struggles not as a fight between parts but as a pain management effort, no one feels left out in the cold and you're less likely to face backlash. As Fisher put it, "Because they successfully dealt with the problem independently of the relationship, neither party feels cheated or angry, and neither is likely to try to sabotage or ignore their agreement. A working relationship is maintained for the future."

Conclusion

But the desire for pain relief is not a sign of being broken—it's a sign of being human.

When everything inside you screams, *You must have that thing!* it can feel difficult or even impossible to stop. Giving up a habit or addiction is like asking your protector parts to jump into a fire with the hope they won't burn. But the desire for pain relief is not a sign of being broken—it's a sign of being human. And if we want to stop problematic behaviors and aim for long-term goals like fulfillment, health, and happiness, we need to work *with* our parts—all of them—instead of fighting them.

Sometimes people ask me, "How long have you been in recovery?" Honestly, I couldn't tell you. While counting days is a valid (and common) strategy, it doesn't work for me. I don't keep track of how many days it's been since I learned to drive—driving is just something I do now. I don't count the days since my last abusive relationship—healthy relationships are just something I have now. My personal preference is to overlay new stories onto the old ones. That's why I love doing circus. The bruises on my body once told the story of trauma. Now they represent my desire to push past what I once thought impossible. But even if you never set foot in a theater, your entire life is performance art. As Shakespeare (also a fellow drug user)* famously wrote:

All the world's a stage
And all the men and women merely players;
They have their exits and their entrances;
And one man in his time plays many parts

Artists turn invisible stories into visible forms. So do addicts. Art demands an audience and invites new ways of thinking. Addiction does the same. Your symptoms are storytellers—and every untold tale inside you deserves your attention. Imagine the possibilities if we learned to *listen* to the survival stories told by our parts rather than judging our parts for trying to survive their stories?

Your symptoms are storytellers.

Bottom-Line Takeaways

1. Addiction is not a binary ("you have it or you don't") but a spectrum onto which all people fall.

2. Desire for pain relief is not the only factor driving addictive behaviors, but it's a powerful one.

3. Most addiction models fail to recognize mind multiplicity.

4. Doing the same things over and over is not a sign of insanity—it's a sign of pain.

5. Addiction is what happens when our desire to avoid pain outweighs our capacity to endure it.

---

* "In the current issue of the *South African Journal of Science*, [researchers] document the presence of cocaine and myristic acid (a plant-derived hallucinogen) in clay-pipe fragments retrieved from the beloved bard's Stratford-Upon-Avon home." https://www.scientificamerican.com /article/shakespeare-on-drugs/

6. Your mind has two branches of its protective division—proactive and reactive.

7. Protective parts don't care about life quality—they care about pain management.

8. Addiction is not a battle between good and evil—it's an effort by your inner world to self-protect.

9. Using negotiation strategies from the business world can help with parts who want different things.

10. Third path thinking focuses not on the part's wants, but the why behind each want.

Action Step Options

I have no time (1–5 minutes):
EXTEND GRATITUDE TO YOUR PARTS.

Set a timer for one minute, then go inside your mind and send out gratitude to all your protectors. You can use your own words or say this: "Thank you, parts, for trying to help me. I don't understand you all yet, but I'm trying. I recognize you all want the same things for me and that we're all on the same team." If you want to extend the practice, continue offering up words of appreciation and gratitude, even if you aren't fully clear on which parts you are addressing.

I have some time (5–15 minutes):
ADDRESS THE FEARS
OF YOUR PROTECTORS.

Do the previous exercise. Then consider your most problematic habit and make a list of all the reasons why your parts are concerned about giving it up. You can use this format or make up your own in your notebook or journal:

My most problematic habit: _____

Five things my parts are afraid will happen if I stop doing this habit:

1. _____

2. _____

3. _____

4. _____

5. _____

I'll make time (15–45 minutes):
ALIGN with polarized parts.

Do both previous exercises. Then, fill in the chart below (or copy it into your journal or notebook). You can use the chart in the **Types of Parts** section on page 33 for help. Do your best *not* to judge or shame yourself for your answers. The goal of this exercise is curiosity and awareness.

Step 1. ALIGN with the "problem" part.

A. Acknowledge.	
L. Listen.	
I. Identify the interests.	
G. Give gratitude.	
N. Name the other part.	

Step 2. ALIGN with the "idealized" part

A. Acknowledge.	
L. Listen.	
I. Identify the interests.	
G. Give gratitude.	
N. Name the other part.	

Step 3. Recognize the interests of both parts

Either think about or write down all the interests of your parts. Look for overlap.

Step 4: Identify your choices

Make a list of all the people, places, and things available to help you.

Step 5: Negotiate a solution

From the list you created in Step 4, choose whatever feels the easiest to do and most beneficial for all your parts. If you get stuck on this step, you can flip to chapter 9 to learn about how to use micro-yeses.

Chapter 6

Are We There Yet?

Self-Parenting Younger Parts

If you stay aligned with your inner child,
you'll always feel forever young.

—**Bhuwan Thapaliya**

Adulting gets a bad rap.

Whether you had an idyllic childhood or a nightmare asylum of a home life, childhood is still a time of powerlessness and dependency. Kids need permission to use the bathroom, must raise their hands to speak, and unless they know how to cook, have to hope that dinner doesn't *again* include the dreaded canned asparagus. Yuck.

For some, childhood evokes happy memories of kickball games and fingerpainting. But for others (me included), it's more of a cringey trip through a pain portal. As a kindergartner, I wanted nothing more than to ride the seesaw. As I watched my classmates soar up and down, feet kicking up clouds of dust with gleeful shrieks, the seesaw seemed the epitome of schoolyard magic. Forget going to Disney—all I wanted was to sit on that rickety, splinter-filled wooden plank*

---

* This was during the 1980s, a time when homes still had lead paint, the *Encyclopaedia Britannica* was our Google, and kids rode with no seat belt in the back of smoke-filled, wood-paneled station wagons.

and fly. But this was an impossible dream. While the shy, often bullied little me was used to doing most activities alone, the seesaw was a two-player game—and the ringleaders of the "We Don't Like Britt" Club (yes, that was a thing) expressly forbade anyone to play with me.

In hindsight, I've come to realize that kids who bully are usually the products of unkind adults. It's easy to write off childhood drama and think, *Well, kids are just cruel.* But this sentiment minimizes both the pain of the person bullied *and* the pain contributing to the bully's behavior. If we don't understand the origin of the pain, cycles of abuse are doomed to repeat.

But I digress. Let's return to the playground. . . .

One scorching September afternoon, fate appeared to smile upon that lonely pigtailed six-year-old. As I sat under a tree reading, the two queen bees of Tackan Elementary School, Ainsley and Masha, looked over at me, snickering to each other and whispering. They then marched up and offered me a deal: "If you stand by the seesaw and watch us today, we'll give you a turn tomorrow." I couldn't believe my luck. Delighted by the sudden turn of events, I jumped up and joined them, obediently standing in place by the seesaw until the clock ran out on recess. *I did it!* I thought triumphantly to myself. *I stood and watched them for the entire hour! It's going to be my turn next!* As the bell rang and kids scattered, I grabbed my Trapper Keeper (the must-have organizer for every 1980s kid) and returned to class, excitedly counting the hours until the next day, when I was sure they'd make good on their promise.

As you might imagine, that didn't happen.

Each afternoon, in what quickly became a daily ritual, I dutifully stood by as the girls seesawed up and down, each time taunting me with their empty promise: "Stand there and watch us today, and tomorrow it's your turn!" As the seasons changed and leaves crunched underfoot, my hope flickered and waned, but still, that little girl stood beside the seesaw, waiting for a turn that never came.

To this day, waiting for my turn (whether I am merging into traffic or standing in line at the grocery store) sometimes triggers that younger part of me. Most people have at least one (if not more) childhood story of feeling rejected, confused, or embarrassed. In chapter 5, we talked about habits and addictions, and how problematic behaviors often stem from unaddressed wounds. Many of those wounds originate in childhood. And while the clichéd trope "Leave the past in the past" continues to masquerade as wisdom, nothing is that simple.

The idea of leaving the past in the past is like saying your late-night meal of hot wings and chili nachos shouldn't affect your stomach in the morning. You'd never tell a friend bemoaning their previous evening's culinary choices, "Well, that meal was all in the past. It shouldn't bother you today. Just get over it. Move on." The food you eat stays inside your body until your digestive system breaks it down. Our minds are the same.

Like food, any experience we "ingest" needs to be metabolized. Otherwise, it can remain in our systems and cause brain indigestion, which manifests as symptoms of anxiety, depression, or any other flavor of stuckness. Rather than trying to erase our memories *Eternal Sunshine**–style, we need a way to connect with our younger parts so the past doesn't interfere with the present.

By approaching your younger parts with curiosity and compassion, you can address past wounds, heal from trauma (even if you don't think you have it), and better trust your decisions. Best of all, by the end of this chapter you'll discover that despite its less-than-stellar reputation, adulting is in fact awesome.

---

* *Eternal Sunshine of the Spotless Mind* is a movie about a woman (Kate Winslet) who undergoes a procedure to erase memories of her former boyfriend Joel (Jim Carrey). Highly recommend.

What Is the Inner Child?

The words *inner child* can spark intense disagreement. Some argue the concept of the inner child is a metaphor, nothing more. Others insist the inner child is simply the result of electrified brain ooze. As is true with the polarizing topic of addiction, there are merits to and problems with the various inner child theories. One of the biggest issues with scientifically proving the existence of an inner child is that you can't quantitatively study it—at least not yet.

Many aspects of the human experience remain unmeasurable. We know love exists, but we can't fully explain it. We know (or at least believe) consciousness is a thing, but the exact mechanisms remain a mystery. And though the Internal Family Systems model is currently designated as an evidence-based practice* (that is, "science says it works"), brain researchers still struggle to explain exactly *why*. So if you're an inner child skeptic, I'll invite you to suspend disbelief as you try the techniques and exercises in this book. And as is true with anything, take what's useful and leave the rest.

Carl Jung is credited with popularizing the concept of the inner child, though the idea can be found across many psychological, philosophical, and spiritual traditions. Some people use the phrase *inner child* to refer to childlike qualities of innocence and wonder. Others use it to refer to your collection of childhood memories. Merriam-Webster defines the inner child as "the childlike usually hidden part of a person's personality" and notes that its "playfulness, spontaneity, and creativity" often go hand in hand with darker emotions that have roots in early life experiences.

Besides being a mouthful of a definition, it's also incomplete.

---

* In 2015, IFS was added to the National Registry of Evidence-Based Programs and Practices (NREPP), a database created by the U.S. Substance Abuse and Mental Health Services Administration.

According to the dictionary definition, the inner child is *one* part of your
mind. But "one child to rule them
all" seems unlikely, since a single part

**Your mind contains
a multitude of inner
children.**

couldn't possibly encompass the totality of *every* experience
from birth to adulthood. From the parts work perspective,
your inner child is not just one part, but many. In other
words, rather than having an inner *child*, your mind contains
a multitude of inner *children*.

Congratulations. You are now in charge of not just one,
but an entire gaggle of inner infants, toddlers, tweens, and
teens, all of whom hold different pieces of your life story.

This news tends to dismay some people at first.

"I already have so much on my plate, and now you're telling me I have to take care of a bunch of people *inside* my
mind, too?"

Well . . . yes. But there's an upside—learning to connect
with your younger parts won't add *more* stress to your life,
it'll reduce it. When you understand what's happening inside your head, you'll spend less time and expend less energy
on ineffective solutions—and you'll also be less susceptible
to wasting money on snake oil scams. One powerful (and
cost-effective) way to align with younger parts is through
a process called *Self-parenting*. Self-parenting is when your
capital-S Self is in charge of your parts, rather than allowing
your parts to roam around unsupervised.

What Is Self-Parenting?

Self-parenting is like regular parenting, but instead of taking
care of little biological organisms (aka human kids), you're addressing the needs, fears, and desires of your younger parts.
Learning to Self-parent can help you access more joy and energy, and it can also help seal cracks where addiction and bad

habits might otherwise sprout. Self-parenting is sometimes referred to as reparenting, but they are not the same:

Self-Parenting: Becoming a parent to your parts. *Everyone* can benefit from Self-parenting.

Reparenting: Going back to the past so you can undo and redo messages and belief systems installed by primary caregivers. Not everyone needs to do reparenting work.

Self-parenting might look like allowing yourself to buy a Star Wars blanket, to eat chicken nuggets for breakfast, or to keep a Squishmallow at your desk. Sometimes Self-parenting means spending quality time with your inner child doing absolutely nothing, and other times it might mean offering words of affirmation or creating time to nap.* While Self-parenting sometimes involves little treats,† it is *not* about indulging or allowing your parts to have whatever they want whenever they want it. To best explain the ideal relationship between your adult Self and your inner child, we'll look at the four parenting styles popularized by psychologist Diana Baumrind in the 1960s. Though her research focused on parenting human children and not inner children, the information still applies—see which one resonates most for you:

STYLE	WHAT IT LOOKS LIKE	WHAT IT SOUNDS LIKE
Authoritarian	Domineering, intimidating, offers little to no validation or encouragement, doles out harsh punishment and sets unrealistic standards.	"Because I said so, that's why."

---

* These examples represent each of the Five Love Languages, popularized by Dr. Gary Chapman. His work refers to couples, but inner children also respond to different types of care.

† "Little treat culture" emerged post-COVID as a trend where you're encouraged to buy small things every time you complete an annoying task.

STYLE	WHAT IT LOOKS LIKE	WHAT IT SOUNDS LIKE
Permissive	The classic "enabling" parenting style. No boundaries, no discipline, overindulging to the point of injury, not considering consequences.	"I'm not a regular mom . . . I'm a cool mom."*
Neglectful	Ignoring problems, not taking time to attend to emotional or physical needs, absent.	"Who cares?"
Authoritative	Setting clear goals and standards but also being supportive and compassionate with efforts. Authoritative Self-parenting encourages growth, prioritizes rest, makes room for mistakes, aims for both a nurturing *and* disciplined approach to life.	"Let's talk about why this task is important and how we can work together to accomplish it."

* *Mean Girls* classic line. SO good.

Authoritative parenting is the optimal style for both internal and real-world parenting. But when you're fused with one of your protectors, as we discussed in chapter 2 (fusion is when a part takes over and Self is no longer in charge), your parts must also play the role of parents. And when parts get stuck parenting other parts, things quickly get messy.

Parts as Parents

Inner Critic: When an untrained inner critic (see chapter 4) oversees your parts, you'll end up yelling at or shaming them *authoritarian* style.

Compulsive or Addicted Parts: When the parts who can't or won't stop a habitual behavior (see chapter 5) take over, you'll notice a *permissive* style.

Safety Parts (fight/flight/freeze/fawn): Chapter 2 discussed the role of your safety parts. Safety parts engage your brain's survival responses to protect you from real or perceived threats. And while safety parts make great bodyguards, they're usually not very good parents:

- If your fight parts are active, you'll be *authoritarian.*
- If your flight parts are active, you'll be *neglectful.*
- If your freeze or fawn parts are active, you'll be *permissive.*

You may default to one parenting style, but it's more likely you'll bounce between all four. The same is true for attachment. Though there are four attachment styles (we'll talk more about attachment in chapter 7), since you have multiple parts, you'll display multiple attachment styles and multiple parenting styles.

If this seems like a snore-a-thon or you feel resistant to the idea of Self-parenting, you're certainly not alone.

Common Objections to Self-Parenting

But I love my parents—do I still need to do this?

Self-parenting isn't about replacing your parents. It's about understanding that adulthood requires what academics call an "internal locus of control," meaning you recognize your own power. Without Self-parenting, you'll stay stuck with an "external locus of control," which leaves you dependent on other people for validation and permission. Self-parenting doesn't devalue your parents' wisdom, but it *does* require you to demote them from the top leadership role to the role of advisor or consultant.

Isn't Self-parenting just a psychobabble way of saying self-care?

Self-care is a trendy wellness term, but it doesn't tell the whole story. Self, as we defined it at the beginning of this book, is the idea that at the center of your core, you have an essence who is bigger than and separate from your parts. Self already has everything it needs. It's your *parts* who need those "unproductive" rest days, walks on the beach, or movie nights with friends. Just like your body parts require different types of care, your younger parts all have varying needs. Self-care might more accurately be called "parts-care."*

But I had to be "the responsible one" my entire childhood. I don't want to deal with kids anymore.

Being forced to nurture adults or take care of siblings is a form of developmental trauma. When children are forced into the role of caregiver, they miss out on childhood perks like innocence and unconditional love.† If you think it's unfair that you had to be responsible as a child, you're not wrong. But even if you were robbed of childhood (I was, too), our younger parts still exist. We have two choices— either Self-parent our parts or let them run wild. Self-parenting can be a chore, but the alternative is worse, since ignoring younger parts creates a massive burden on our minds, moods, and relationships.

---

* Using this logic, technically self-parenting should be called parts-parenting, but Self-parenting has a better ring to it, so I'm making an executive decision to keep it as is.

† Unconditional love is appropriate only in an adult–child relationship. All adult relationships require conditions.

I don't want to do the "therapy thing" of blaming my parents.

Self-parenting doesn't require you to blame your parents. While traditional psychotherapy will inevitably include an exploration of family dynamics and the ways in which your parents' choices and behaviors impacted you, Self-parenting isn't about your parents—it's about *becoming* a parent to all your younger parts.

But I had a happy childhood. Why should I care about doing this?

Having a great childhood doesn't exclude you from the benefits of Self-parenting. Here's why everyone, regardless of their origin, might want to consider giving these techniques a go:

- If you had a difficult childhood, Self-parenting helps you to heal from the effects of it.
- If you had a happy childhood, Self-parenting helps you access the energy, playfulness, and creativity you experienced during that time.

Self-parenting doesn't require a debate about your parents' intentions or an argument over whether a childhood trauma should count as trauma. Even if you had perfect parents (there aren't any), *no one* can protect a developing child from the pains of becoming a fully grown person. Childhood is a time of constant change; every young person goes through periods of powerlessness and struggle. While human development is a massive topic that we won't even attempt to cover in depth here, the following chart gives you a *very* abbreviated list of younger parts, along with their core needs and tasks:

AGE	CORE NEEDS	CORE TASK
0–2 (infancy)	Nourishment, safety, bonding, attachment, sensory stimulation	*Trust:* "I need to know you'll be there."
2–4 (toddlerhood)	Exploration, language development, communicating, consistency	*Boundaries:* "I need to be able to say no."
5–10 (early adolescence)	Competence, belonging, structure, learning to identify and express feelings	*Labeling:* "I need to be able to describe what's happening."
10–13 (tweens)	Independence, peer relationships, identifying likes and dislikes, communicating, friendships	*Independence:* "I need to start doing things by myself."
14–18 (teens)	Identity exploration, autonomy, social connections, purpose	*Differentiation:* "I need to know I can be different from my parents."

Even though your mind contains parts from every age and stage of your development, you won't need to work with all of them. Your physical body doesn't require you to pay attention to every cell, organ, and tissue. For example, you pay attention to your left infraspinatus only if you're an athlete or injured. (I have a torn shoulder right now, which is the only reason I know that the infraspinatus muscle even exists.) You probably don't give your right pinkie finger a second thought—unless you slam it in a car door.

Parts work is similar.

While it can be fun to explore our inner landscape just because it's there (10/10 recommend), your injured or distressed parts are the ones who require attention. These parts can manifest in various ways, often in response to triggers or challenging situations. Like a person confined to an inhumane prison system, your parts do not do well when locked in a cage with unmet psychological, physical, and emotional needs.* Signs that one (or more) of your inner children is struggling and needs attention include the following.

Ten Signs of Wounded Child Parts†

Irrational Emotions

When your emotional responses to an event seem bigger than the severity of the event, that's a sign of a wounded younger part. What people often call overreactions would be better labeled "younger reactions," since there's no such thing as an irrational feeling. Your parts hold stories to which your conscious and logical mind might not have access. When you react higher than a 5 on a scale of 1 to 10 (assuming the problem is mild), that's a clue Self-parenting is needed.

Fear of Abandonment

In the psychological world, you'll hear the expression "Adults can be left, but not abandoned."‡ Relationships are a biological need, and extreme feelings of grief are normal reac-

---

* Interestingly, Sweden's prison system, which focuses on humane treatment and rehabilitation, boasts shockingly successful statistics, as opposed to the American system. Google "Scandinavian prisons" if you want to feel better about humanity.

† Some of these signs can be attributed to neurodivergence, medical issues, or some other origin besides a wounded younger part. This information is a guide, not an "every time for every person" diagnosis.

‡ Source unknown.

tions to relationship loss. But abandonment is different from loss—abandonment implies danger. If you were abandoned as a child, you didn't have the power or resources to protect yourself. When you're a child, abandonment is dangerous. But assuming you're able to meet your basic needs, feelings of abandonment—and the terror that accompanies it—is a sign of an activated child part.

Chronic Loneliness

The problem of loneliness can't be fully solved with relationships. Yes, we are wired for connection, and we need one another. But you can be surrounded by family, friends, coworkers, and community and *still* feel lost in a black hole of despair. If you've solved for relationships and still feel a nagging emptiness, that's a sign of internal disconnection. Poet John O'Donohue advised that "the solution to loneliness is solitude," meaning sometimes we need to retreat from other people to do the work of inner alignment.

Self-Destructive Behaviors

If you notice patterns of behavior like defiance, aggression, withdrawal, or substance misuse, such behaviors suggest one or more of your younger parts is struggling. These behaviors can take various forms, from explosive outbursts reminiscent of childhood tantrums to retreating into sulking silence. However, the consequences in adulthood can be far more serious. When a child-sized part has a meltdown in an adult-sized body, watch out.

Indecisiveness

Hesitation or fear of decision-making, especially in the case of nonlethal situations, can indicate a fearful younger part of yourself needs help. This fear may stem from childhood experiences in which choices were made for you or when your decisions were met with criticism or punishment. Fear of making the "wrong" decision isn't always tied to younger parts but is often the underlying factor.

Constantly Worrying about Disappointing Your Parents

If disappointing your parents equaled danger when you were a child, this fear can persist into adulthood, influencing decisions and behaviors as you strive to meet their expectations. Fear of disappointing your parents can lead to feeling constantly inadequate, guilty, and anxious. The behaviors we call people-pleasing often began with parent-pleasing.*

Recurring Nightmares or Difficulty Sleeping

While medical or environmental issues can contribute to sleep disturbances (and should always be ruled out first), difficulty sleeping, whether it manifests as insomnia, restless nights, or disrupted sleep patterns, is sometimes a signal that inner child parts need attention and care. For many people, the bed is a battleground where unheard stories, "irrational" fears, and big feelings from younger parts rush to the surface.

Fear of Getting in Trouble

No one likes to be on the receiving end of criticism or discipline (excluding those who enjoy safe, sane, and consensual fetish play). I remember asking a former boss to add a smiley emoji to his ominous "come to my office" texts, since I always assumed those texts meant, "I'm about to fire you." If you find yourself unduly anxious about receiving criticism or discipline—such as fearing severe consequences for small errors—it suggests the heightened state of alert of a younger part.

---

* Original author of "people-pleasing started with parent-pleasing" unknown.

Difficulty Setting Boundaries

If you find yourself consistently saying yes to things you don't want to do or allowing others to cross your boundaries, it may be a sign your inner child parts are seeking validation or approval from others. When you were a child, asserting yourself might have led to disapproval or punishment. A childhood fear of upsetting your parents can lead to boundary difficulties as an adult. So if you struggle to prioritize your needs and feel uncomfortable about disappointing people, one or more of your younger parts might need some assistance.

Chronic Dissatisfaction

Feeling persistently unsatisfied or restless despite external successes or achievements may suggest that your inner child is seeking fulfillment or validation from sources outside yourself. Striving for growth and improvement is healthy; feeling perpetually dissatisfied no matter how much you have or do is not. When you find yourself in a never-ending cycle of needing to be, do, or have more, or if you never feel personally satisfied, it's safe to assume a younger part needs you.

While mindset advice continues to dominate the wellness world, the solution to this dilemma isn't to get in your right mind—it's **to get in your right size.***

What does it mean to be right-sized? Being right-sized means your emotional age matches your chronological age. When you struggle with road rage, personal hygiene, procrastination, the maintenance of boundaries, or decision-making (or any of the signs listed), that's an indicator that you've fused with a younger part. This is a psychological state called emotional

Being right-sized means your emotional age matches your chronological age.

---

* Being right-sized is a principle used often in the Alcoholics Anonymous twelve-step recovery program.

regression. Emotional regression, most simply put, is the experience of "I don't feel like an adult right now."

How to Reverse Emotional Regression

Causes of emotional regression can vary widely, from major stressors to minor inconveniences, and we all experience it on a spectrum of intensity. The process of reversing regression is the same whether you're dealing with an inconsequential annoyance or a code red trauma response. I'll give you an example from a very unpleasant experience I had at the dentist.

Note: Trigger warning—the situation I'm about to describe involves sexual trauma.

Most people dread dental visits. While we can all agree it's not particularly enjoyable to have someone poking around in your mouth with sharp objects, for some people (me included), a trip to the dentist goes beyond mild discomfort to full-blown panic. Not all "I don't want to go to the dentist" resistance is related to trauma or emotional regression. But one very common (and rarely discussed) side effect of trauma, particularly sexual trauma, is dental anxiety. Because I survived sexual trauma during both my childhood and adulthood, trips to the dentist historically created very big problems for my system.

After years (like, a *lot* of years) of neglecting my teeth and gums, I finally had to face the dragon. After several disastrous tries with unskilled and unkind providers, I found a wonderful dentist who moved slowly, answered questions, and made sure I felt safe during procedures. But even with a snuggly weighted blanket, sunglasses, and soothing music, I was still afraid when I had to lie down and submit to the scalpel-wielding, mask-wearing tooth doctor. In the middle of a routine visit, I suddenly felt a familiar surge of panic—along with all its usual accoutrements like a racing heart, shaky legs, and feelings of impending doom. As my eyes welled up, I had to work *very* hard to keep myself from leaping up, knocking over the hygienist, and running out the door.

But despite my panicky state, I was able to Self-parent through the moment, choosing to stay in the chair and let the dentist proceed with the necessary work. This is a state of emotional regression I call *conscious fusion*. Conscious fusion is when you're not in your right size but still have enough access to your adult Self to navigate the situation. It's not an ideal state, but it does allow you to hang on until conditions improve.

If you want to reverse emotional regression and return to your right size, you'll first need to identify in which of the three emotional regression states you're stuck:

States of Emotional Regression

Conscious/Fused

You're aware that regression is happening, but you're able to maintain a window of tolerance and make choices in the moment.

Example: Sitting in that chair, I did *not* feel like my most capable adult Self. But my choice power was still available in spite of the panicky feelings—I was conscious of my choice to ask the dentist to pause or stop, but instead I decided to cope with the situation until I could take my newly shined-up teeth home.

Note: The important thing to know about conscious fusion is that it is **choice-based** symptom management. Nothing is getting solved, but you're aware of and can consent to what's happening in the moment.

Conscious/Defused

You're able to observe your parts, listen to their stories, and reverse the regression.

Example: After successfully completing the dental visit, I could have managed my discomfort by going back to bed or zonking out with Netflix (both totally acceptable solutions). But since this was the third panic-filled visit in a row, instead of symptom management, I decided to take time to ALIGN with my activated younger part (*acknowledge, listen, investigate, give gratitude, negotiate*), so I could better understand the story under the symptoms. It took a few attempts (and several visits to my therapist) to work through things, but eventually my dental phobia switched from debilitating panic to a more manageable level of regular dental anxiety, and I haven't had a panic episode since.*

Note: Conscious fusion is *symptom management*, while conscious defusion is *problem resolution*.

Unconscious/Fused

You're unaware that regression is happening, and you feel confused and out of control.

Example: Before I understood parts work, dental visits created torrents of panic, anger, and emotional outbursts. I felt broken and ashamed of my inability to tolerate a simple teeth cleaning.

So . . . if there's conscious/fused, conscious/defused, unconscious/fused . . . what about unconscious/defused?

You can't be unconscious and defused. Defused, by definition, means you have awareness of and can respond to your parts rather than feeling collapsed under them. Since defusion requires consciousness, being both unconscious and defused is impossible.

When you put all the different states together, you get what I call the **Emotional Regression Matrix**.

---

* Shout-out to Dr. Kelly Thomas, DDS, for being the best dentist ever.

The Emotional Regression Matrix

REGRESSION STATE	FUSED	DEFUSED
CONSCIOUS	Quadrant 1: "I'm managing the situation." This is a symptom management approach. It can look like: • Choosing to cope with a distressing moment until it passes • Implementing a soothing parts-care strategy • Choosing to dissociate or numb out	Quadrant 2: "I'm no longer activated by the situation." This is a problem resolution approach. It can look like: • Using ALIGN or other skills to meet your part's underlying needs • Listening to the stories told by the symptoms • Managing the symptoms *and* addressing their root cause.
UNCONSCIOUS	Quadrant 3: "I have no idea what is going on with this situation." This can look like: • High reactivity • Withdrawing from people • Impulsive behaviors • Mood swings	Quadrant 4: It's not possible to be both unconscious *and* defused. Pretend this box doesn't exist.

When you find yourself in quadrant 3 of the Emotional Regression Matrix—feeling reactive, impulsive, and disconnected—it's helpful to have a set of tools so you can transition back to quadrant 1 or quadrant 2. But before we dive into the next set of techniques, let's pause here for a second and review the terrain we've covered. We've demystified the idea of the inner child and discussed Self-parenting (what it is, why it matters, objections to the work. We've decoded the signs of wounded younger parts and discussed the different types of emotional regression.

In the next section, you'll learn strategies to help you return to your adult-sized Self.

How to Reverse Emotional Regression

There are four steps to reverse an emotional regression:

- **Recognize** you're in a regression.
- **Review** your state of regression.
- **Reflect** on your choices.
- **Reach** for a Self-parenting tool.

Recognize You're Stuck in a Regression

While understanding root causes of emotional regression can be useful, instead of starting with "Why is this happening?" a better use of emotional bandwidth would be to first ask yourself, "How old do I feel right now?" If you're totally frazzled and genuinely have no clue what's happening in the moment, you may need to first DEFUSE, as discussed in chapter 2 (*describe your physical sensations, exit the room, feel your body, use your sense, shift, exhale*).

After you defuse, take a minute to consider how old you feel. When I was sitting in that dentist's chair, my first step was to identify the approximate age I was experiencing—the activated part of me felt like a five-year-old. You don't need to pinpoint a specific age, but you can use the table of ages from earlier in this chapter as a guide:

AGE	CORE NEEDS	CORE TASK
0–2 (infancy)	Nourishment, safety, bonding, attachment, sensory stimulation	*Trust:* "I need to know you'll be there."
2–4 (toddlerhood)	Exploration, language development, communicating, consistency	*Boundaries:* "I need to be able to say no."
5–10 (early adolescence)	Competence, belonging, structure, learning to identify and express feelings	*Labeling:* "I need to be able to describe what's happening."
10–13 (tweens)	Independence, peer relationships, identifying likes and dislikes, communicating, friendships	*Independence:* "I need to start doing things by myself."
14–18 (teens)	Identity exploration, autonomy, social connections, purpose	*Differentiation:* "I need to know I can be different from my parents."

Review Your State of Regression

What are my choices right now? Once you recognize your general age range, then look at the Emotional Regression Matrix and see where you land. If you're in quadrant 1, you'll still be regressed but able to cope with the situation. If you find yourself in quadrant 3, say to yourself, "I am stuck in an emotional regression right now. My parts are scared. This is a thing." Affirming your experience and labeling it as a regression helps you create space, so you don't feel as mindfused. At the dentist, I was able to locate myself in quadrant 1. When I got home, I used Self-parenting and therapy to land in quadrant 2.

Reflect on Your Choices

One of the most efficient ways to get unstuck—from anything—is to ask yourself, "What are my choices right now?" Whenever your brain is conscious of your choices, it'll be less reactive. And a less reactive brain means your safety team won't need to bombard you with fight/flight/freeze/fawn sensations. In any given moment, you might not *like* your choices, but often, even *thinking* about your choice points can be enough to halt a regression. During my dental procedure, I told myself over and over, "I can choose to stop. I can choose to stay. I can choose to pause." Awareness of choices allowed my system to tolerate the situation until it was over.

Reach for a Self-Parenting Tool

It's important to match your intervention to your activated part's age. Something that might work for a teenage part won't be developmentally appropriate for an infant part, so you can use the following list as a guide (or make up your own).

AGE	CORE TASK	SELF-PARENTING STRATEGIES
0–2 (infancy)	*Trust:* "I need to know you'll be there."	Soothing activities like taking baths or covering yourself with blankets or soft clothes. Sitting by the water or outside. Rocking or listening to binaural beats or any other nonlyrical music.
2–4 (toddlerhood)	*Boundaries:* "I need to be able to say no."	Find something or someone you can say no to. Safely find things to throw outside. Scribble angrily with chalk or finger paint and make a mess.
5–10 (early adolescence)	*Labeling:* "I need to be able to describe what's happening."	Use the 5-4-3-2-1 technique: Identify and say out loud five things you can see, four things you can hear, three things you can touch, two things you can smell, and one thing you can taste.
10–13 (tweens)	*Independence:* "I need to start doing things by myself."	Call a friend. (If you don't have any, go to a coffee shop or grocery store and interact with the people there.)
14–18 (teens)	*Differentiation:* "I need to know I can be different from my parents."	Listen to loud music, go for a drive, scroll on your phone, look at funny memes or videos, make plans with friends.

The strategies outlined in the above table are designed to help with symptom management so you can catch your breath in quadrant 1 (conscious/fused). Sometimes coping strategies are enough to fully reverse a regression and put you back in quadrant 2, where you'll feel right-sized again. But when symptom management alone doesn't get the job done, you may need to use ALIGN. After I made it safely home, I turned off my phone and computer, grabbed a notebook, and connected with my younger part:

ALIGN Step	How It Worked
A: Acknowledge your availability.	"Hello, little Britt. I know being at the dentist was super scary. We're home and safe now, and I'm available to listen to you."
L: Listen.	During this step, my part told me how overwhelmed she felt having a "big person" staring down at her, how much it hurt, and how scary it felt.
I: Investigate.	After asking this part a few questions, I realized the triggered feelings at the dentist felt like what she'd experienced during a traumatic event—powerlessness, smallness, pain, fear.
G: Give gratitude.	"Thank you, little B, for sharing this with me. I'm not mad at you and you're not in trouble. I'm so glad you are here."
N: Negotiate.	The incident uncovered by my inquiry felt too big for me to work through alone, so I negotiated with my part that she would not have to do any more dental or medical visits until we could schedule a session with our therapist.*

* Not everyone has the choice to go to therapy. If a trauma-informed therapist is not available to you and you are struggling with sexual trauma, RAINN is the nation's largest anti-sexual violence organization, and they offer free resources. See https://rainn.org/national-resources-sexual-assault-survivors -and-their-loved-ones.

The goal of parts work and Self-parenting isn't to eliminate emotional regression altogether. No matter how much inner healing, wellness practice, or daily meditation you log, it's human nature to regress to younger parts from time to time. You don't need to worry that you're not doing the work if you regularly feel the slip and slide of emotional time travel. The task isn't to prevent regression, but to recognize it and then safely find your way back home to your Self.

Conclusion

Once you know how to connect with your younger parts, you'll discover how fun it is to have them around. Slogging through the tasks of Self-parenting unlocks an entire world of giggly, mischievous, and playful parts of your mind. With consistent care and connection to your Self, your inner children become entertaining little travel companions.

Adults are often quick to see the world as it is; they hurry through their days without a second glance. But children see the world as it could be—a tree becomes a fortress teeming with fairies; a lake is an enchanted swampland ruled by sea monsters. I get why the trend of "I don't want to adult today" became a viral sensation. It's tempting to romanticize childhood and long for its simplicity.

But I wouldn't trade being an adult for anything.

But I wouldn't trade being an adult for anything.

Granted, adult life isn't always sunshine and rainbows. Things like paying taxes, figuring out childcare, dealing with mounting medical bills, and worrying about a geopolitical apocalypse are ever-present concerns. Intense pain and challenges dot the landscape of even the most resourced and financially secure adults.

And.

Despite the challenges of grown-up life, I prefer the agency of adulthood to the dependency of childhood. When you were a child, your social circle was likely confined to classmates and neighbors. As an adult (assuming you have your basic needs met and access to choices), you get to choose where to live, what to wear, and to whom you wish to spill your secrets. Unlike children, who are subject to the whims of authority figures and societal norms, as adults, *we* get to choose whom and what to let into our "weird little worlds," as Robin Williams's character famously remarked in *Good Will Hunting*.

As an adult, you can wear a Halloween costume in June, and if you want to buy a birthday cake on a day that *isn't* your birthday, you don't need permission. (Buying a birthday cake for yourself when it's not your birthday is a fun adult flex. I encourage you to give it a try.)

Just as I made the decision to suit up for circus life, as an adult, you get to explore your own passions and curiosities; you can opt in to your own side quests. Your younger parts are standing at the door of your mind, eagerly awaiting your return.

And now, if you'll excuse me, I have a date with my inner child to go play on the seesaw.

Bottom-Line Takeaways

1. Even the best childhoods include a degree of pain and powerlessness.

2. You can't leave the past in the past.

3. Rather than having one inner child, you have a family of inner children.

4. Self-parenting younger parts can help them feel seen, safe, and understood.

5. Self-parenting is appropriate whether you had a good childhood or not.

6. Self-parenting isn't about blaming your parents— it's about becoming a parent to your parts.

7. Wounded younger parts make themselves known through symptoms like indecision and difficulty with boundaries.

8. When you feel younger or smaller than your chronological age, you're in an emotional regression.

9. Recognizing you're in a regression is the first step to reversing it.

10. Being an adult is awesome.

Action Step Options

I have no time (1–5 minutes):
PICTURE YOUR PARTS.

One of the easiest ways to stay connected to your younger parts is to have a daily reminder that they exist. If you have access to your childhood photographs, put one of them as your phone or your computer screen.

I have some time (5–15 minutes):
TALK TO YOUR PICTURE.

Do the exercise above, then take some extra time to talk to the little you in the picture. You can talk to them out loud or in your head. If talking feels too strange, you can also write them a letter telling them everything they wished someone would have said to them.

I'll make time (15–45 minutes):
ALIGN with your inner child part.

Complete the first two tasks, then put ALIGN into action. Think of a recent situation where you felt emotionally triggered and consider approximately how old you felt. Once you've identified an age range, either think about or copy your answer into your journal or notebook.

ALIGN Step	What It Sounds Like (write in or think about what's true for you)	What This Does
A: Acknowledge your availability.		Defuses you from your younger part. You are not your younger part, and your younger part is not you.
L: Listen.		Let the part know you want to hear what's on its mind. Then listen to what it has to say.
I: Investigate.		Ask clarifying questions to make sure you fully understand your parts' feelings and the nature of the situation.

ALIGN Step	What It Sounds Like (write in or think about what's true for you)	What This Does
G: Give gratitude.		Extending gratitude inward allows for nervous system regulation and access to your "thinking brain," and keeps you out of the fusion states of fight, flight, freeze, or fawn. We talk a lot about the power of extending gratitude *out*. Less talked about but equally powerful is extending gratitude *in*.
N: Negotiate.		Negotiating a solution with your parts does the same thing as a negotiation at work. When all parties feel heard, compromises are easier to land on, and when all parties feel like they are getting some of their needs met and all their needs heard, things tend to coast more smoothly.

Part Three

Parts Work in Action

In Part Three, we'll explore how to apply parts work. We'll look at how your parts interact with other people's parts and how these dynamics shape your relationships. You'll discover how to unlock your creative power, leading to a more authentic and empowered life. Finally, we'll tackle what to do when you feel stuck, showing you how to move forward without needing motivation.

Chapter 7

The Relationship Equation

When Your Parts and Other People's Parts Collide

> *Whenever two people meet,*
> *there are really six people present.*
>
> —**William James**

W hy won't he just grow up already?" Gretchen grumbled, kicking off her shoes and grabbing a fidget spinner from the coffee table in my office. As she settled on my couch, her anger gave way to sadness. Absent-mindedly twirling the toy between her fingers, she recounted her partner Lee's frequent (and rowdy) happy hours with friends, video game binges, and neglect of their home and dogs. She genuinely loved Lee, and while their first three years together had felt seamless and easy, the past two had been a different story. Though there was no physical or emotional abuse in the relationship, Gretchen nevertheless felt hopeless about the future. "It's like having a teenager," she lamented. "I feel more like a parent than his partner. Is this what a relationship is supposed to be?" she inquired. Without waiting for an answer, frustration rising in her voice, she continued, "It's like he doesn't even consider me at all. And somehow I *still* show up and give and give and give. What's *wrong* with me?"

Gretchen's dilemma isn't uncommon. I hear versions of this story every day in my office.

Sometimes I think life would be so much easier if we could teleport ourselves to another planet, one where the population consisted of puppies and plant babies in lieu of people. Alas, science tells us we need connection with other humans—relationships are not optional. But whether it's friends who dump their trauma on us, colleagues who monopolize conversations, or partners who avoid childcare, even reasonably functional relationships can be tricky.

It's for these everyday relationship pains that parts work best applies.[*]

What we call communication problems are often *parts* problems.

What we call communication problems are often *parts* problems. After all, if you don't know how many people are *really* in the room during a conflict, even highly logical solutions might fail. Have you ever had an argument with someone and wondered, *Are we even speaking the same language?* Or *Who is this person in front of me right now?* Parts work doesn't provide an automatic fix, but it does explain why conflict sometimes feels so baffling and infuriating. When two people clash and things don't seem to add up, that's because relational math doesn't math like you'd expect.[†]

Bottom line?

The relationship equation is this: **Me + You = More Than Two.** (Like, *way* more than two.)

---

[*] Any type of couples therapy (including parts-focused couples therapy) is not recommended if there is abuse or active addiction present in the relationship.

[†] Sometimes the relationship math doesn't add up because one person is gaslighting or manipulating the other. These are not the situations to which this information applies.

During any interaction with another human life-form, all your parts and all *their* parts can end up on a collision course. You might notice yourself (and others) cycling through a variety pack of behaviors, depending on the context and the people involved. You can guarantee that in any relationship dyad, besides the capital-S Selves of the two people present, there are also at least three other groups of parts hovering close by:

- **Wounded younger parts** (including child parts who might feel scared and small, toddler parts who are subject to tantrums, and teenage parts who might act sullen and moody)
- **Proactive protectors** (parts who want to prevent harm by controlling or pleading)
- **Reactive protectors** (parts who respond to harm by distracting or numbing)

In the story on the previous page, when Lee loafed on the couch with a gaming mic cemented to his head, his teenage parts appeared to dominate the situation. In reaction to his adolescent regression, Gretchen could have stepped back, considered her options, *then* chosen how she wanted to respond to Lee. But instead, when Lee's reactive parts bared their teeth, Gretchen's own parts flared, frantically whispering, *If he doesn't get off the couch, you'll end up divorced and broke, everyone will laugh at you, and your dog will be out on the street. MAKE HIM GET UP!* And for the past two years, Gretchen tried to do just that—nagging, yelling, and scolding, but to no avail. The more she hounded Lee, the more his teenage parts dug in their heels and refused to budge. By the time she ended up in my office, she felt so burned out and resentful she was ready to walk out on the relationship.

Even if you are fortunate to have no high-level drama or all-night shouting matches in your relationships, you might still feel annoyed, confused, and exasperated by the people in your life. In this chapter, you'll learn parts work strategies to manage the relationships you have, and ways to build the ones you want. First, we'll talk about attachment, a powerful undertow that can tank even the best relationships. We'll also challenge commonly held beliefs about friendship, work relationships, and intimacy, and you'll get new ways to think about each. Finally, you'll leave this chapter with a toolbox of practical tips and tricks you can use to manage any relationships in your life. Here's an at-a-glance look at the road map:

1. Attachment styles

2. Challenging relationship norms

3. Relationship toolbox

Warning: Even though it's ideal for two people in a relationship to be on the same page, I'd encourage you *not* to leave this book open on your friend's, colleague's, or partner's desk with highlighted passages and sticky notes urging them to do their parts work and get their sh*t together. While you can always ask someone to participate in personal growth exercises, we ultimately can't control other people. But if you don't have a willing partner to accompany you on your parts work adventure, don't despair. Understanding your own parts can still help your relationships *and* the encounters with random people you'll meet in the wild—whether they recognize their own multiplicity or not.

With that, let's jump in.

Attachment Styles (You Have More Than One)

A discussion about relationships is incomplete without a visit to the land of attachment, since attachment is often the unseen source of friction between friends, coworkers, and partners.

Once you join forces with any human in any context, everyone's parts come out to play—and not all of them play by the same rules. If you're familiar with attachment theory, you may have heard of the four attachment styles originally outlined by psychologists Dr. Mary Ainsworth and Dr. John Bowlby. The four styles are **secure**, **anxious**, **avoidant**, and **disorganized**. Here's an overview:

Traditional View of Attachment

ATTACHMENT STYLE	HOW IT LOOKS	HOW IT SOUNDS
Secure Attachment	Comfortable with closeness and solitude, healthy boundaries, communicates effectively, can form stable and trusting relationships	"I'd be sad if things ended, but I'm okay with or without this relationship."
Anxious Preoccupied Attachment	Seeks excessive reassurance, overly dependent, high levels of anxiety and emotional volatility, difficulty with trust	"You can't leave me. I'm not okay without you."
Anxious Avoidant Attachment	Avoids closeness, maintains distance, downplays the importance of relationships, and prefers self-reliance over connection	"I don't need or want anyone. I'm okay only if I'm on my own."

ATTACHMENT STYLE	HOW IT LOOKS	HOW IT SOUNDS
Disorganized Attachment	Displays erratic and unpredictable behavior, struggles with trust and intimacy, has a fluctuating and contradictory approach to relationships	"I'm not okay with you, and I'm not okay without you. I want you to come closer and I want you to go away."[*]

* There's a book about borderline personality disorder called *I Hate You—Don't Leave Me* . . . a title that perfectly encapsulates the disorganized attachment style.

Even though attachment theory originated in the 1960s, the model continues to be a star player in the psychology world. It exploded in popularity through the work of Dr. Amir Levine and Rachel Heller with their book, *Attached*. Rabid fans devoured attachment content as quickly as it appeared. The resurgence of the theory in pop culture created a flood of trending hashtags, memes, online quizzes, and kitschy merch (including hats that read *Anxious Avoidant*). In an interview about why attachment received hundreds of millions of hits on the intergooglewebs, Levine had this to say: "There's a lot less you can tolerate when you are faced with imminent harm than when the world feels generally safe. . . . Seismic shifts happened to a lot of people in their relationships during the pandemic. Some close relationships, be it friendships or romantic ties, or at the workplace, dissolved, and new close ones formed. . . . A very important principle in attachment science is that periods of increased threat or danger can lead to activation of the attachment system."[*]

Attachment theory originally focused on the relationship between caregivers and infants or young children, emphasizing the importance of early interactions. Levine and

* "Attachment theory is trending on TikTok. Here's why, according to the Columbia professor who wrote the book on it": https://tinyurl.com/yuc67snm.

Heller added an important contribution to the existing pool of knowledge, showing attachment is not just a childhood phenomenon but one that continues throughout our adult development. All experiences from bassinet to blue-haired bliss shape our attachment patterns. And as the world continues to rapidly change, understanding how to build and sustain healthy relationships is non-negotiable.

But there's a catch: attachment theory doesn't take the multiplicity of mind theory into consideration.

You don't have one attachment style—you bounce between all four.

From the parts work perspective, you don't have one attachment style—you bounce between all four. Within the vastness of your interior world lies the capacity to express *all* the attachment styles, with your different parts exhibiting different patterns depending on the relationship. Tempting though it may be to categorize and neatly organize our minds, human relationships are too complex and nuanced to be reduced to a single style of relating. If it's true we all have multiple personalities, it makes sense we'd also have multiple attachment styles. Your parts take turns hopping in and out of the driver's seat, each veering toward a different attachment style.

ATTACHMENT STYLE	WHO'S LIKELY IN CHARGE	HOW IT LOOKS IN RELATIONSHIPS
Secure Attachment	Self	"I'd be sad if it ended, but I'm okay with or without this relationship." • Relationships tend to flow smoothly. • Conflict is handled skillfully. • Healthy boundaries are in place.

ATTACHMENT STYLE	WHO'S LIKELY IN CHARGE	HOW IT LOOKS IN RELATIONSHIPS
Anxious Preoccupied Attachment	Younger parts	"You can't leave me. I'm not okay without you." • Relationships tend to include power struggles. • Patterns of emotional regression, dependency, emotional volatility, and fear of abandonment are exhibited. • There are no boundaries.
Anxious Avoidant Attachment	Protector parts	"I don't need or want anyone. I'm okay only if I'm on my own." • Relationships tend to be absent. • Patterns of isolation, shutdown, and withdrawal are exhibited. • There is stonewalling instead of healthy boundaries.
Disorganized Attachment	Polarization (see chapter 5) between younger parts seeking closeness and protector parts pushing for distance, creating erratic behavior and push-pull dynamics	"I'm not okay with you, and I'm not okay without you. I want you to come closer and I want you to go away." • Relationships tend to be chaotic. • Conflict styles alternate between flexing up and shrinking down. • There are shifts between good boundaries, no boundaries, and stonewalling.

A better question to ask than "What's my attachment style?" is "What's my attachment style in this relationship?" You might feel totally Self-led and secure at work, but anxiously preoccupied when your friends don't answer your texts. You might feel avoidant when it comes to forming close friendships but disorganized in romantic partnerships. Gretchen, whom you met in the introduction, displayed anxious preoccupied attachment with Lee, but an inventory of her *other* relationships yielded a surprising mix of the four styles. Here's how they looked:

ATTACHMENT STYLE	WHERE IT SHOWED UP FOR GRETCHEN	WHAT IT LOOKED LIKE/PARTS INVOLVED
Secure	At work	Gretchen feels confident and capable at her banking job. She enjoys her coworkers and clients, and even though the workplace has its stressors, she usually feels like her Self and can set boundaries and manage the ups and downs of hectic days.
Anxious Preoccupied	With Lee (her husband)	Gretchen is worried if she doesn't nag Lee, something bad will happen to him and their marriage will fall apart. Gretchen's anxious preoccupied parts compel her to play the parent role with Lee. She struggles to set boundaries, taking on all the household tasks.

ATTACHMENT STYLE	WHERE IT SHOWED UP FOR GRETCHEN	WHAT IT LOOKED LIKE/PARTS INVOLVED
Anxious Avoidant	With friends	Because all her energy is zapped worrying about Lee, Gretchen distances herself from friends. Her avoidant parts compel her to avoid socializing, a decision she justifies by telling herself, "I'm just too busy." Instead of setting boundaries, Gretchen stonewalls her friends by ghosting them and ignoring invitations.
Disorganized	With her sister (Anna)	Gretchen wants to be close to her sister Anna, but most interactions result in Anna's shaming or criticizing Gretchen's life choices. Gretchen feels torn by parts who want to hug it out, parts who want to duke it out, and parts who want nothing to do with her sister at all. Sometimes Gretchen maintains her boundaries, sometimes she has none, and sometimes she shuts down and stonewalls Anna, depending on the day and situation.

At the end of this chapter, you'll have an opportunity to do an attachment inventory, too, but if you want to pause and skip straight to it now, feel free to do so and then return here when you're ready.

Otherwise, let's keep this relationship ball rolling.

Now that you have a grasp of the multiple nature of attachment, we'll look at parts work principles in three categories of relationships—friendships, colleagues, and intimate partners. We'll challenge commonly held beliefs and examine alternatives. We won't cover family stuff here, but if you're interested in family dynamics, there's a chapter in my first book, *The Science of Stuck,* titled "The Emotionally Unskilled Family," which covers ten common family struggles—and what to do about them.

Challenging Relationship Norms

What might be considered normal behavior in one culture could be seen as unusual or unacceptable in another. And even norms within a culture evolve over time. When I was a raging chain smoker in high school and college, it was normal to light up everywhere. Until the 1990s, smoking was permitted in airports, restaurants, bars—even hospitals. Now it's prohibited in most places. If you're in the twelve-step recovery world, you'll bump into the saying " 'Normal' is just a setting on your washing machine."* Something might be considered normal,† but that doesn't mean it's good. What's normal for a sociopath would be considered objectively bad by most standards. (Yes, that's an extreme example, but you get the point.)

---

* Original source unknown.

† The concept of normalcy is also limiting and exclusionary, often leading to marginalization of people or groups who deviate from the perceived norm, whether due to differences in identity, ability, behavior, or other factors.

Normal is *not* a synonym for healthy. With that in mind, let's look at a few commonly held beliefs in relationships. Then we'll consider how you can repurpose these norms by using the power of parts work.

Rethinking Friendships

Some people view friendships as a luxury, and many adults walk around without any friends at all. (I was one of these people for years.) However, the science of attachment proves friendships are a biological necessity—we need them to thrive. But what does *friend* really mean? We use the same term for both sandbox playmates and lifelong allies, despite the dramatic differences between these relationships. This one-size-fits-all approach to friendship reasonably creates confusion, because the rules of friendship that worked fine for us as children no longer make sense when we are adults.

Common belief: *Friends should be forever.*

Why this is a problem: The idea you need to stay friends with someone because "We've been friends for so long" ignores a fundamental truth—people change, and so do their parts. The mix of parts you experienced last month, last year, or ten years ago differs from today's combination. We don't expect our body parts to stay the same over time (the body you had as a five-year-old in no way resembles the meat-suit you walk around in now), and the same is true psychologically. The belief that friends should be forever can keep you stuck in unhealthy or less-than-ideal friendships, diverting energy that could be better spent nurturing more aligned connections.

Alternative view: A friendship is a living, breathing organism comprising two Selves and countless parts. Like all carbon-based life-forms, friendships follow a cycle—birth, sprout, bloom, wilt, die, rebirth. This sounds morbid, but accepting the ever-changing nature of friendships makes it less jarring when they run their natural course. Even if your parts and your friend's parts manage to grow and evolve together, feelings of deep grief and loss are normal responses to changing friendship dynamics. You may have parts who desperately want to hang on to their friends forever or parts who protest any change in a relationship's status—but when you know how to Self-parent, as we talked about in chapter 6, you can better guide your parts through the process.

Takeaway: *It's okay to outgrow your friends.*

Common belief: *You should have only deep, meaningful friendships.*

Why this is a problem: Limiting yourself to one type of friend is restrictive. It fails to acknowledge the diverse assortment of friendship preferences held by your different parts. As we discussed in chapter 2, nature needs biodiversity to sustain life. Similarly, *social diversity* can help your internal ecosystem thrive. Requiring your friendships to all fit into the same category is a setup for letdown.

Alternative view: Not all friendships need to exist at the same level of depth and intensity. It's beneficial to consider having a mix of different types of friends:

Ride-or-die friends: These are level-ten soul-connection friends, available at three a.m. in a crisis. They are deeply connected to you, and you know you can count on them for anything.

Work friends: The people with whom you chat between meetings might never be close friends, but they make work more enjoyable and provide professional support.

Activity friends: These are the people whom you join for travel, sports, or hobbies. You don't need to have deep conversations with them (or even like them very much), but they're fun to hang out with within the context of the activity.

Nostalgic friends: Trips down memory lane are more fun with friends—even if you don't currently share any interests. These friends are fun to connect with occasionally when you want to revisit old experiences.

Online friends: Online friends with whom you chat or interact count, even if you've never met in person.

Takeaway: *It's beneficial to have different types of friends.*

Common belief: *Friends should hold you accountable.*

Why this is a problem: Asking someone to hold you accountable creates a dynamic where your friends must take responsibility for your parts' actions and progress (or lack thereof). This can lead to resentment or an overinflated sense of responsibility. Accountability requires you to manage your own parts; no one can truly hold you accountable except yourself. Relying on friends for accountability outsources the job of parent and creates a power differential that may lead to unhealthy dynamics and negative outcomes.

Alternative view: While friends can offer support and encouragement, accountability is about the relationship between your Self and your parts. Friends create the container for you to share goals and progress. They provide a safe ear for you to be honest about your struggles. Friends can help you keep *yourself* accountable, but the job of a friend is neither to parent your parts nor to police your actions. This alternative provides mutual respect and equality within the friendship.

Accountability is an inside job.

Takeaway: *Accountability is an inside job.*

Rethinking Work Relationships

It wasn't *that* long ago you'd be expected to show up at work and leave your feelings at the door. While that norm was unhealthy and unrealistic, it seems the pendulum wildly overshot its mark, landing at the equally unhelpful extreme of bringing *all* your feelings to work. I've heard many high-level leaders declare, "The future of work is human." And while this trend is preferable to its antiquated opposite of treating workers like machines, if the future of work is human, it helps to know how human brains work, especially when it comes to relationships. Bringing all your parts to work is both unnecessary and unsafe. With this in mind, let's unpack three work relationship norms—and what you can do instead.

Common belief: *You should be totally authentic at work.*

Why this is a problem: Being fully authentic and vulnerable at work is ill-advised. Sharing too much personal information about your parts or revealing your parts' deep vulnerability with unsafe or unskilled people can lead to misunderstandings, misuse of information, or emotional burnout. It can also blur professional boundaries and create an unsafe environment.

Alternative view: Instead of sharing every part of yourself, you can curate a group of parts who would be most useful to bring to work. You don't need to expose all parts of yourself to be a good team member, colleague, or manager. Sharing *some* parts of yourself is necessary, but giving an all-access pass to your inner world creates an unhealthy and unsustainable work environment. Even well-meaning and interested colleagues might not be able to handle your retelling of a traumatic story. Instead, when you consciously choose which parts get to come to work, you contribute to a healthier and psychologically safer environment for everyone. You can use my SAFE assessment (yes, another acronym) to decide whether to share at work:

S: *Structured:* Organize your thoughts purposefully to ensure clarity and boundaries.

A: *Appropriate timing:* Ask for consent, and make sure the receiver is in a good space to listen.

F: *Familiarity:* Consider the depth of your relationship and their receptiveness to your share.

E: *Emotional readiness:* Assess your own emotional state and preparedness to manage potential reactions before you share.

Takeaway: *You need to bring only some of your parts to work— not all of them.*

Common belief: *Workplaces are families.*

Why this is a problem: When people are told by companies that they're part of the family, it creates unrealistic expectations, confuses younger parts, and blurs professional boundaries. The metaphor of work as a family can also be quick to trigger unaddressed family-of-origin wounds. In a family, relationships (ideally) are deeply personal and loving, while workplace relationships are designed primarily to be professional and transactional. If your parts believe your workplace is your family, they might overidentify with the company and have difficulty leaving if you feel the job no longer fits. High-control religions use "we are your family" as a manipulative tactic to maintain members' loyalty despite bad behavior from those at the top, and well-intentioned workplaces can accidentally do the same.

Alternative view: Workplaces should foster a supportive and collaborative environment, but they are *not* families. Professional relationships can be friendly and supportive without crossing into familial territory. Clear boundaries and professional respect are crucial for a healthy work environment. If you want to use a metaphor, replace the family one with a sportsball analogy: your colleagues are not your family, but you can think of them like an athletic team focused on a shared goal. This can create a positive culture without the complications of expecting coworkers to behave like siblings or managers to function as parents. If your parts long for a sense of family and your biological family is not an option, it is preferable to view your friends, rather than your workmates, in that role.

Takeaway: *Companies are not families. You do not owe them the same consideration you'd give a family member.*

Common belief: *You should show only your positive parts at work.*

Why this is a problem: The belief that you should display only your positive parts at work can place undue pressure on different parts of you, particularly those who are already stressed or struggling. This expectation can lead to internal conflict, where parts feel they must suppress valid emotions like frustration, sadness, and fatigue. Ignoring these feelings can result in burnout, resentment, and a disconnect between your true self and the persona you present at work. This discord can be particularly challenging for parts who have experienced similar pressures in past environments, whether at home or in previous jobs.

Alternative view: It's important to recognize that all parts of you have valuable perspectives and emotions. Instead of forcing positivity, acknowledge and validate all your parts. This can involve taking moments throughout the day to check in with your parts, attempting to understand their needs and addressing any discomfort. Creating a work culture that accepts the natural ebb and flow of human expression can reduce the internal pressure to be constantly upbeat. Encouraging self-compassion and realistic expectations helps your parts feel seen and respected, leading to more genuine engagement and productivity.

Takeaway: *Positivity at the expense of authenticity can create problems. A better solution is to create internal space for all your parts to exist.*

Rethinking Intimate Relationships

When it comes to intimate relationships, one size does *not* fit all. Thankfully, you don't have to search hard to find books, podcasts, and blogs to help you navigate intimate relationships of every conceivable form—monogamy, consensual non-monogamy, asexual partnerships, kink . . . and more. The rules of intimacy change dramatically depending on which form your relationship takes and the preferences of the people involved, but there are a few time-honored parts-work-based principles that universally apply.

Common belief: *No one can love you until you love yourself.*

Why this is a problem: Because your mind contains so many different parts, it's unrealistic to expect yourself to always love *all* of them. A consistent state of "I love myself" does not sustainably exist (unless you're on psychedelics, but those do eventually wear off). You can adore some parts of yourself but struggle to accept others. And relationships are sometimes the vessel needed for parts to heal. The love from healthy partners helps mirror back to us our own lovability (with the caveat that partners are *not* parents, and it is ultimately *our* responsibility to Self-parent our parts). If we all had to wait for perfect love and perfect trust before attempting intimacy, there would be no relationships at all.

Alternative view: While you *don't* need to love all parts of yourself to be in an intimate relationship, you *do* need to know how to Self-parent before it's safe to enter a partnership without risking codependency. The word *codependent* is often used to describe either the enabling partner of someone with an addiction, or someone who caretakes others and neglects their own needs. Now, I'm not a big fan of the term *codependent*. It can be blame-y and makes it sound like we don't need other people—and we do. But since that word seems to have staying power, I define it like this:

Codependency is an effort by *your* inner child parts to rescue someone *else's* inner child parts.

If you dig beneath the surface and look at the function of codependent behavior, you'll likely find a lost and terrified inner child part who believes if they can only fix/control/heal someone else, everything will be okay. Codependency is not solved by relationships—it is solved by Self-parenting your parts and setting healthy boundaries.

> **Codependency is an effort by *your* inner child parts to rescue someone *else's* inner child parts.**

Takeaway: *You don't need to love yourself before someone else can love you, but Self-parenting skills help prevent codependency in romantic relationships.*

Common belief: *Closure requires two people.*

Why this is a problem: Believing you need closure from someone else can keep you stuck in painful or unhealthy situations. Closure is not always possible, especially in complex or abusive situations. And closure is off the table completely if the person with whom you have conflict suddenly disappears or dies. Waiting for the perfect closure conversation can lead to prolonged suffering, as it places the power of your healing in someone *else's* hands. This belief can prevent you from taking the necessary steps to heal and move forward with your life.

Alternative view: Closure is a necessary step to heal and move forward, but you *don't* need it from an external source. Instead, think of closure as an *internal* process—closure is about the connection between your Self and your parts. If another person is unavailable and unwilling to have a closure conversation, your Self can always be a resource to help wounded and grieving parts feel their feelings, accept the reality of the loss, and readjust to a life without the other person in it.*

Takeaway: *Closure is a necessary step—but it doesn't require another person.*

Common belief: *My partner should meet all my needs.*

Why this is a problem: Believing that your partner should meet all your needs places unrealistic and excessive pressure on them and on the relationship. All your different parts have varying emotional, social, and practical needs, so the expectation that one person can fulfill all of them is neither fair nor realistic. This belief can lead to disappointment, resentment, and dependency. It can also strain the relationship by ignoring the importance of Self-parenting and multiple support systems.

Alternative view: Healthy relationships include partners who support each other while *also* recognizing the importance of building *other* sources of fulfillment. We want to have multiple streams of connection, and that requires us to assemble an array of friends, family, hobbies, and personal interests. Diversifying our portfolio of relationships reduces the likelihood that one person will feel overburdened by unrealistic expectations.

Takeaway: *Multiple streams of support are preferable to just one.*

Relationship Toolbox

Now that we've challenged the beliefs and provided alternative ways of thinking about friendships, work, and intimate

---

* The tasks of feeling feelings, accepting the loss, adjusting to the new reality, and moving forward are based on Harvard psychologist J. William Worden's *model of the four tasks of grief*, the gold standard of grief work that better explains the process of grief and loss than Elisabeth Kübler-Ross's theory of the five stages of grief. Kübler-Ross developed this model based on people dying from cancer.

relationships, let's move on to the parts work relationship toolbox:

- Relationship Antagonists and Anchors
- How to Apologize
- Pass the Mic

You can use these strategies to help improve your current relationships and to keep in mind as you seek to build new ones.

Relationship Antagonists and Anchors

The first set of tools identifies behaviors guaranteed to get *everyone's* parts suited up for battle. These are the things *not* to do—I call them the five relationship antagonists.

RELATIONSHIP ANTAGONIST	WHAT IT IS (AND WHY IT'S A PROBLEM)	WHAT TO DO INSTEAD
Always (and never)	Using absolute statements such as "you always" or "you never" in communication can cause parts to feel defensive. It's rare that someone always or never does or says something.	Avoid all-or-nothing statements and use more flexible language, like "*Sometimes* I get frustrated when I see/hear _____" or "*I've noticed a pattern* of _____, and about that I feel frustrated."

RELATIONSHIP ANTAGONIST	WHAT IT IS (AND WHY IT'S A PROBLEM)	WHAT TO DO INSTEAD
Accusations	Placing blame and creating a hostile atmosphere in relationships by assigning fault. Accusations tend to trigger reactive protector parts.	Use "parts of me" statements, like "When I perceive my opinions aren't being heard, it triggers anxiety and frustration among my parts. I'd appreciate it if we could find ways to ensure everyone feels valued in our conversations."
Assumptions	Coming to unfounded conclusions about motives or intentions, leading to misunderstanding.	Use "parts of me" statements, like "I noticed we haven't talked in a few days, and some of my parts are worrying if I've done something wrong or if we're drifting apart. Our connection means a lot to me, and I want to make sure we're both feeling good about it. Are you available to talk?"
Avoiding	Steering clear of difficult conversations or conflicts, prolonging issues and fostering resentment among everyone's parts.	Instead of avoiding difficult conversations, confront them directly with openness and honesty. Make sure the other person consents to the conversation.

RELATIONSHIP ANTAGONIST	WHAT IT IS (AND WHY IT'S A PROBLEM)	WHAT TO DO INSTEAD
Aggression	Using verbal or physical aggression, which damages trust, undermines safety, and causes lasting harm.	Set a timer if needed, and structure the conversation so that if either person feels too fused with their angry parts to skillfully continue the conversation, you can immediately stop.*

* In abusive relationships, this is not always possible. Reminder: Abuse is not a communication problem, a parts problem, or a relationship problem. Abuse is an abuser problem, period.

By recognizing (and avoiding) the five relationship antagonists, you lay the groundwork for healthier, more fulfilling connections. Antagonist behaviors create relational decay and hinder attachment efforts. Instead, you can use what I call the five relationship anchors.

RELATIONSHIP ANCHOR	WHAT IT IS (AND WHY IT'S GOOD)	HOW TO DO IT
Acknowledge	Recognizing and validating the feelings and perspectives of your partner. This helps prevent them from fusing with protector parts and biting you.	Say, "I understand that parts of you feel upset because of the recent changes at work. That makes sense."

RELATIONSHIP ANCHOR	WHAT IT IS (AND WHY IT'S GOOD)	HOW TO DO IT
Appreciate	Expressing gratitude and recognition for your partner's efforts. This helps prevent defense parts from jumping off the bench into the discussion.	Regularly thank your partner for their support and specific actions. "I appreciate how you support me even when some of your parts are unsure about how I'm feeling or why."
Ask	Seeking to understand your partner. Asking genuine questions helps keep their logical team engaged and prevents their safety team from sounding the alarm.	You can say, "I really want to make sure I'm hearing you, and parts of me need clarification. Can you please tell me again what this was like for you?"
Attend	Paying attention to your partner in the moment. When people (and their parts) feel seen, they're more likely to settle.	Put away distractions, like your phone, and make eye contact while your person is speaking.
Adapt	Showing flexibility and willingness to change, which helps their parts feel like you're collaborating with them, rather than fighting them.	Be open to trying a new solution or thinking about a problem from your partner's perspective. You can say, "Parts of me are hesitant, but I'm willing to try."

To best demonstrate how the next two skills can be applied in real-life situations, we'll use Gretchen and Lee from earlier in this chapter as examples.

How to Apologize

Description: The surprising secret to repairing relationship wounds is this: *don't* apologize. While the words *I'm sorry* are fine for minor relational bumps and bruises, apologies are about the feelings of the person who *caused* the harm, rather than the experience of the person on the receiving end. When someone apologizes, it becomes the burden of the *hurt* person to manage the feelings of the *hurtful* person. Instead of apologizing, you can offer up an amends, a practice popularized in the twelve steps of Alcoholics Anonymous.

How to do it: You can use the model I adapted from the ninth step of amends making. I call it the four Os of relationship repair.

1. **Own** what you did ("I admit I said/did . . . That was wrong of me.")

2. **Observe** how your behavior impacted the other person ("I imagine you must have felt . . .")

3. **Outline** your plan to avoid repeating the behavior ("In the future I'll prevent this by . . .")

4. **Offer** to listen ("Is there anything I missed you want me to understand? I'm listening.")

Example: Even if Lee didn't change or own his own behavior, it still wasn't a good look for Gretchen to yell and call him names. After storming out of the living room once again, Gretchen took a few deep breaths, returned to Lee, and said the following (notice the absence of the words *I'm sorry*):

Own: "Lee, I admit I called you names and yelled at you. That was wrong of me."

Observe: "I imagine you must have felt angry and disrespected."

Outline: "I am working on this in therapy and in the future will try to use my skills before coming at you."

Offer: "I want to understand what this was like for you. Did I miss anything? If there's anything you'd like me to know, I'm willing to listen."

Important: When you use this strategy, you are not deferring blame to your parts or bypassing your responsibility to manage their feelings. It is *not* a viable repair strategy to say, "Sorry, but my angry parts decided to come out and take over my brain." If you want your partner to know why the situation triggered your parts, you can return to the conversation later. Repair is about seeking to understand your partner, not an effort to be understood *by* them.

Pass the Mic

Description: When your Self leads a conversation, you can maintain a state of emotional regulation (see chapter 2). From this state, you can speak on *behalf* of your parts instead of letting them take over the conversation. Think of this like a boxer who starts yelling at his opponent after receiving an illegal below-the-belt punch. The referee puts his hand out and urges the injured boxer to retreat to his corner. Then the referee takes the microphone and communicates the situation to the audience. In this circumstance, the referee is the

Self and the boxer represents the parts. When one of your parts gets hurt, you need your inner "referee" (Self) to take the microphone and communicate, rather than letting the part do the talking.

How to do it: The defusing technique you learned in chapter 2 is necessary before you'll confidently be able to pass the mic. First, exit the conversation as quickly as possible. Then find a quiet space and take a few minutes to DEFUSE.

D: Describe your physical sensations.

E: Exit the room.
(You can skip this step, since you'll have already exited the triggering situation.)

F: Feel your feelings.

U: Use your senses.

S: Shift your body.

E: Exhale.

After you defuse, imagine asking your part to pass the mic over to you before you engage in further conversation with another person. Let the part know you understand their feelings and assure them you'll keep their interests in mind as you return to the conversation.

Example

When Gretchen came home from work and saw Lee on the couch, she noticed anger surging through her body and knew it was a bad idea to have a conversation in this state. She dropped her bags on the counter and went upstairs, where she invested a few minutes in paying attention to her body sensations, feeling her angry parts, using her senses to notice the smells and sights around her, gently stretching her body, and exhaling slowly. Once she felt defused, and her angry part had passed the mic back to her Self, she could then return to Lee and have a skillful Self-led conversation.

Conclusion

Gretchen's frustration with Lee wasn't just about his behavior. Even if he had thrown away his video game console, scooped poop without complaint, and quit drinking altogether, Gretchen *still* would have found reasons to be dissatisfied. Why? As she explored her inner world, Gretchen uncovered a trapdoor leading to smaller parts who felt terror during her alcoholic father's wild mood swings. While Lee's choices were certainly not conducive to a functional adult relationship, Gretchen was able to recognize and attend to her scared and neglected younger parts. This enabled her to approach Lee from a more curious, adult, and calm place.

I'd love to tell you that Lee had his own epiphany and decided he should probably talk to someone, but it was more shock at Gretchen's changed behavior that made him think, *WTF is this parts work stuff?* If you can't inspire the people in your life to venture inward, feel free to poke at their curious or competitive parts. It doesn't matter *how* they get through the door—all that matters is that they *do*.

Regardless of whether you're in an intimate relationship, your parts are bound to pop up with friends, coworkers, and all the people you'll meet along the way. And while yes, we all need relationships to thrive, you already exist as a whole being, with a fully installed Self. In his book *You Are the One You've Been Waiting For*, Dr. Richard Schwartz observes, "Another kind of happiness exists that you can feel steadily whether you are in a relationship or not. It comes from the sense of connectedness that happens when all your parts love one another and trust and feel accepted by your Self."

Easier said than done. But well worth the effort.

Bottom-Line Takeaways

1. Communication problems are often parts problems in disguise.

2. The relationship equation is this:
   Me + You = More Than Two.

3. Any difficult conversation likely includes wounded younger parts and protective parts.

4. The four attachment styles are secure, anxious preoccupied, anxious avoidant, and disorganized.

5. Since you have multiple parts, you can also have multiple attachment styles.

6. The rules of friendship that applied in childhood don't translate into adulthood.

7. You don't need to bring all your feelings to work.

8. You can love parts of yourself and still struggle to accept others.

9. It's your job to Self-parent your parts. No one can do it for you.

10. When we speak on behalf of our parts, communication flows more smoothly.

Action Step Options

I have no time (1–5 minutes)

Before attempting relationship interventions (or conversations) of any kind, it can be helpful to do it from a *defused* state. You can do this in your head, or copy the acronym DEFUSE into your journal or notebook and write about it:

D: Describe your body sensations.
E: Exit the room.
F: Feel your feelings.
U: Use your senses.
S: Shift your body.
E: Exhale.

After you DEFUSE, check in with yourself to see if you feel a little more regulated and spacious, or slightly less activated. Repeat if desired.

I have some time (5–15 minutes):
ATTACHMENT INVENTORY

ATTACHMENT STYLE	WHAT RELATIONSHIPS TRIGGER THIS STYLE?
Secure	
Anxious Preoccupied	
Anxious Avoidant	
Disorganized	

I'll make time (15–45 minutes)

Do the other two exercises and then ALIGN with one of your parts who currently feels activated by either a friendship, work relationship, or intimate partnership.

ALIGN Step	Write your response *to* and/or what you hear *from* your activated part.	What This Does
A: Acknowledge your availability.		Defuses you from your parts. You are not your parts, and your parts are not you.
L: Listen.		Inquiry allows your Self to lead and gives you more information so you can then make an appropriate decision about what to do next.
I: Investigate.		Ask clarifying questions to make sure you fully understand your parts' feelings and the nature of the situation.
G: Give gratitude.		Extending gratitude inward allows for nervous system regulation and access to your "thinking brain" and keeps you out of the fusion states of fight, flight, freeze, or fawn. We talk a lot about the power of extending gratitude *out*. Less talked about but equally powerful is extending gratitude *in*.
N: Negotiate.		Negotiating a solution with your parts does the same thing as a negotiation at work. When all parties feel heard, compromises are easier to land on, and when all parties feel like they are getting some of their needs met and all their needs heard, things tend to coast more smoothly.

Chapter 8

Becoming More You

Unlocking Your Creative Power

Each of us is an artist of our days;
the greater our integrity and awareness, the more
original and creative our time will become.

—John O'Donohue

I wanna go *hoooooooooooooome*," wailed a tired, hungry, cranky little voice. "This is *borrrrrrrrrrring*."

I couldn't really blame her. For the past three hours we'd been wandering around a maze of swords, portraits, and pottery. To me, this museum visit was a chance to finally witness things I'd only read about or seen in movies. To her, every room of statues looked the same, every tapestry-covered hallway an exercise in drudgery. And don't get me started on the medieval paintings of the Madonna and child.* Each time we passed one of their strange-looking faces, she'd look up at me with pleading eyes, begging, "Can we *go* now?" Meanwhile, the sun outside was shining almost mockingly compared to the stale air and gray walls.

---

* In an article on *The Collector*, Zoe Mann says, "In Medieval art, baby Jesus had the body of a baby but the face of a fully-grown man. Today, this can be very shocking and even hilarious. However, back in Medieval times, this was a typical depiction of baby Jesus in Medieval religious iconography." https://www.thecollector.com/baby-jesus-in-medieval-religious-iconography/.

Eventually I gave in. "Okay." I sighed. "Let's go." I gently took her hand and led her outside. After gulping down fresh air and a quick snack, she made a beeline for the grassy park, where she eagerly threw down her backpack and jumped up on the monkey bars.

If you haven't guessed by now, that voice wasn't from an actual child on a field trip—the "get me out of here" cry was courtesy of five-year-old Britt, who had long surpassed her limit of good-for-you adult activities. She doesn't like museums. Not one little bit.

I used to feel embarrassed by and angry with parts who didn't like what I thought they should like—art museums topping that list. My college-aged parts think they *should* stand in awe before the Renaissance classics. My impostor parts think they *should* spend hours carefully taking notes and memorizing facts so they can sound smart to snobby people. But my little parts don't care—they want nothing to do with dusty old relics* created by dusty old people, and they quickly get bored and fidgety.

Even if you're someone who adores museums, maybe you can relate to the feeling of doing an activity you think you should like but don't. Or being someplace you should want to be, but nevertheless counting the minutes until you can get the heck out of there. When it comes to your chosen activities, do you ever feel like there's a checklist you need to follow? You're not alone. I don't know what person high atop which mountain decreed, "You're an adult now, so you have to like these things," but here's a common *should list*—you may recognize a few:†

---

* My adult parts understand why museums are important. I'm not anti-museum.

† *Disclaimer:* Sometimes the list of shoulds includes things legitimately necessary for well-being. This includes moving our bodies to whatever degree is available, eating, staying hydrated, and being open to new perspectives. It's often important to do what we should even if it's uncomfortable or unpleasant. But this chapter is not about those things.

- You should read classic literature.

  There's a common belief that we should *enjoy reading Tolstoy or Dostoevsky. There will never be enough time to read everything even if you try, so while the classics can be great, read what you want. (And you can always watch the movie versions.)*

- You should like gourmet food.

  The idea that we should *enjoy fine dining can create unnecessary pressure. While I appreciate the efforts of food scientists, the molecular gastronomy people can keep their salmon foam and foie gras powder. I'll take a slice of New York pizza, please and thank you.*

- You should want to travel.

  Glitzy vacation photos splashed on social media promote the idea that we should *have a passion for traveling. But that might not be your thing. There's nothing wrong with you if you don't enjoy traveling.*

- You should enjoy parties.

  Many people feel they should be extroverted and enjoy social gatherings, even if they are naturally more reserved. As a hard-core neurodivergent introvert myself, I'm familiar with this dilemma.[*]

- You should have a high-powered career.

  The pressure to aim for a prestigious or high-earning job can be strong, as it's often equated with success and ambition. While mainstream Western society says we should *all want to be a boss or an entrepreneur, those roles may not align with how you want to do life.*

---

[*] I've perfected my own version of Brexit, mastering the art of exiting parties.

- You should start a family.

  Many feel that by a certain age, they should *get married and have children. As someone child-free by choice, I'm often asked why I didn't have kids or told I'll regret my decision. Yet it would be considered horribly rude if I walked up to a parent and said, "Why did you have kids? You're going to regret that decision."*

- You should love the outdoors.

  Fact: Nature is good for us. But not everyone gets their kicks hiking or camping. If you're not an outdoorsy person, you're allowed to pursue activities that better fit your lifestyle.

Life's "good for you" tasks aren't the endgame. So what's the point of this discussion? As was true in the case of my experience at the museum with five-year-old Britt, you might have parts who resist societal expectations and crave different experiences. We're often so busy trying to achieve a perfect score, it's easy to forget life's "good for you" tasks aren't the endgame. If you want to become more of who you are and less of who you were told you should be, then your parts' quirky fantasies, whimsical ideas, and plain old "because I feel like it" impulses demand consideration. And that's what this chapter is about—how to stop the storm of shoulds so you can feel more like your Self.

And beware—we're going to talk about creativity and play, two topics that tend to cause more anxiety and discomfort in grown people than the Sunday scaries.* But before we examine whether creativity is synonymous with art (it isn't)

---

* Sunday scaries are sometimes physiological. (If, for example, you've spent all weekend trying to downshift out of work mode, your body knows it's about to blast off at ninety miles per hour the next day and therefore produces stress hormones.) But often the scaries are parts of you who need attention. You can use the ALIGN method if you struggle with end-of-weekend anxiety.

and debate if play is an adult necessity (it is), let's start with one of the biggest shoulds of all—the idea that you should cultivate spiritual practices and beliefs.

Spirituality is one should-do item to which I enthusiastically subscribe.

Now, I realize you might be thinking, *But you just told me **not** to should on myself!*[*] And you're right. So why do we need to talk about spirituality in a book about parts work (and why should you listen to a therapist's opinion about it)?

Simplifying Spirituality

What *is* spirituality? It's frequently described as a sense of meaning or purpose, a belief in God or the universe, or a feeling of awe. Sometimes spirituality is a sense of transcendence. Other times it might be a bond with animals or nature. Some people feel spiritual when visiting certain buildings or locations, watching a sunset, or listening to the sound of water. To make this concept as broad and inclusive as possible, here's the definition I use:

> *Spirituality is anything that helps you feel **connected**. Period.*

If we're defining spirituality as a sense of connection, the list of potential practitioners expands to include therapists, the person who lets you merge into traffic during rush hour, your FedEx delivery driver, and anyone with a pulse. And the list of spiritual places extends beyond prescribed locations to include everything above and below, inside and out.

---

[*] World-renowned psychologist Dr. Albert Ellis, founder of REBT (rational emotive behavior therapy) in the 1950s, coined the phrase *"Don't 'should' on yourself."* He also invented the term *must-erbation* to describe the demands we place on ourselves.

As Dalai Lama XIV put it, "There is no need for temples; no need for complicated philosophy. Our own brain, our own heart is our temple; the philosophy is kindness."* Under this umbrella, there's room for every conceivable religious, spiritual, and philosophical orientation and symbol system.

Studies show spirituality can boost immunity, improve mental health outcomes, and extend longevity. But before you roll your eyes at the idea of an athleisure-clad cuddle puddle, let's first clarify: spirituality *doesn't* have to look like what we were taught it should. While burning incense, chanting, or adhering to religious doctrines can be perfectly acceptable choices, spirituality might also be as unique and personal as your favorite playlist.

But there's a parts work plot twist (of course).

While spirituality is often viewed as a connection to something *outside*, parts work expands the concept to include connection with what's *inside*. When you defuse from and align with your parts, you embody what Internal Family Systems calls the "eight Cs of the Self"—compassion, curiosity, clarity, creativity, calmness, confidence, courage, and connection. When you operate from Self, you're walking a spiritual path. This is why, despite popular opinion, it is good to be "full of your Self."

But I thought it was bad to be full of yourself. Wouldn't that make me a narcissist?

People fused with and dominated by narcissistic or arrogant parts aren't full of themselves—they're profoundly disconnected from themselves. When we're filled with Self, we don't act out in thoughtless or unkind ways. Quite the contrary. The more Self-energy we access, the more tolerance and compassion we can extend to

---

* *The Dalai Lama: A Policy of Kindness: An Anthology of Writings by and About the Dalai Lama.*

other people. As you read in the introduction, Self is the I in the storm, the center of your wheel, the mysterious soul stuff connecting everyone to everything. The aim of spirituality isn't to deny your Self, it's to unlock *more* of it.

DIY Spirituality

Spiritual practices are at their most potent when they're viewed as opportunities instead of obligations. But myths about spirituality fly around as fast as the algorithm will fling them at us, so it's tough to know where to start. If spirituality is just a fancy-schmancy word for connection, then we can clear up a few misconceptions. Here are my top eight:

Myth: **Spirituality requires religion.** Religion is generally defined as the worship of God or the supernatural through an institutional system of attitudes, beliefs, and practices. But spirituality is about *connection*, which may or may not include religion.

Myth: **Spirituality means you must believe in the unseen.** If we're running with the "spirituality is connection" definition, belief in supernatural or invisible entities isn't mandatory. Spirituality can be grounded in personal growth, human relationships, and mindfulness practices.

Myth: **Spiritual people are always peaceful and happy.** The intent of spirituality is to help us cope with the discomfort of our humanity, not for us to bypass it and become robots. Not all behaviors or expressions of feelings are acceptable, but all feelings are valid. Spirituality does not require you to deny your feelings.

Myth: **Spirituality means rejecting material wealth.** During my cult days, we were discouraged from working outside the compound (I did anyway). The leaders preached the value of rejecting material things and embracing poverty. For some people, that approach works. But spirituality is expansive enough to peacefully coexist with material abundance.

Myth: **There's a correct way to be spiritual.** If we exclude abuse or coercion, there's no right or wrong way to feel spiritually connected. Spirituality can take on a near-limitless form of beliefs, practices, and experiences.

Myth: **Spirituality requires you to kill your ego.** Your ego is a valuable part of your inner society; you don't need to kill it. Your ego protects you from being inundated with stimuli, it helps filter out unnecessary noise, and it provides a sense of identity and structure. Instead of trying to eliminate your ego, the goal is to stay defused *from* it rather than being dominated *by* it.

Myth: **Spiritual experiences must always be profound or mystical.** There's a misconception that spiritual experiences must be a psychedelic trip through time and space. They *can* be. But spirituality can also exist in simple, everyday moments of humaning like skipping rocks on the lake or doing the dishes.

Myth: **To be spiritual, you must have a leader.** Spiritual growth doesn't require others to believe what you believe, and it doesn't require someone to lead you. Mentorship and guidance can often be useful, but spirituality is a deeply personal experience. Ultimately, our journey into this world (and out of it) are solo expeditions—we can't outsource the job.

In the next section, we'll talk about using rituals to connect with your parts. The word *ritual* sounds mysterious, but it's simply a set of actions performed in a specific sequence for a predetermined reason. Using rituals can help turn even basic life tasks from meh to magical.

Parts Work Rituals

Rituals are everywhere. In his book *Ritual: How Seemingly Senseless Acts Make Life Worth Living*, anthropologist Dimitris Xygalatas writes, "From knocking on wood to uttering prayers, and from New Year celebrations to presidential inaugurations, ritual permeates every important aspect of our private and public lives. . . . There is something about high-arousal rituals that seems to thrill groups of individuals and transform them into something greater than the sum of their parts."[*] Anthropologists and sociologists who study rituals describe four different types—magic, religious, substantive, and factitive.[†]

TYPE OF RITUAL	WHAT IT IS	EXAMPLES
Magic	Magic rituals are intended to influence outcomes in the physical world and/or supernatural forces.	Burning sage, lucky charms, not changing your socks during basketball season
Religious	Religious rituals are meant to honor, worship, or communicate with deities or spiritual entities.	Prayer, sacraments, and worship services

---

[*] https://www.ethicalsystems.org/why-humans-thrive-on-rituals/.

[†] Specifically, these categories can be linked to the theories and writings of scholars such as Arnold van Gennep, Émile Durkheim, and Victor Turner.

TYPE OF RITUAL	WHAT IT IS	EXAMPLES
Substantive	Substantive rituals help define and uphold the core values and beliefs of a community or institution.	Secular holidays such as Mother's Day, Father's Day, Memorial Day, Labor Day
Factitive	Factitive rituals mark the transition to a new role or status.	Inauguration ceremonies, graduation, military commissions, retirement parties

This list can be limiting, so I'll add a fifth category—*connective rituals*. These are *any* practices that strengthen the bond between yourself and/or other people. You don't need to buy any special tools or create elaborate ceremonies to do connective rituals (though you can if you want). We'll take a break from all this theory chatter and look at practical examples in a minute, but first, here's a quick overview of the components of rituals:

Intention: *Why* are you doing the ritual?

Setting: *Where* are you practicing the ritual?

Objects: *What* can you use to assist you?

Structure: *How* are you going to implement it?

With these questions in mind, you can create deeply personal and effective rituals to connect with your parts.

Practical Magic

While academics define *magic rituals* as an attempt to control the natural or supernatural world, it does feel rather magical to connect with parts. (I thought my first IFS therapist was a sorcerer in disguise.) But connective rituals aren't intended to influence *external* outcomes; they're designed to build a better relationship with your *internal* system. Four types of connective rituals we'll cover here are **transitions, celebrations, creativity,** and **play.** And be forewarned: your protector parts might resist these practices—or flat out refuse to do them at all. That's a perfectly reasonable (and expected) response. Instead of shaming yourself or forcing yourself through these rituals, see if you and your parts can agree to try one or two exercises from earlier in this book. Once you've had a few reps in the mental gym building your ALIGN muscles, return to this section and give it a go.

One important caveat with rituals—you don't necessarily feel any different while you do them or after you finish. In fact, sometimes you might feel worse. Remember, your brain is wired for pattern-seeking and prediction-making—throwing rituals into the mix can initially feel very uncomfortable and unpleasant. But it's more important to *do* the ritual than to feel a particular way while doing it. Sometimes I don't see or feel the benefits of rituals until days or even weeks after I practice them.

Transition Rituals

As we jump through life's hoops to pay the bills, do the chores, and hoard the toilet paper, it can be confusing for parts to know where, when, and even *who* they are. Transition rituals can help your parts feel more grounded, and thus less likely to fuse and cause problems. Child psychologists often recommend transition rituals for kids, because these practices can help with emotional regulation, orient the child in time and space, and help with expectations management. Because many of our parts are child-aged, transition rituals can also be useful for adults.

Transition ritual: *Inner Child Bedtime*

Why it's good: Bedtime rituals for children enable their nervous systems to downshift out of go mode. These types of rituals can facilitate secure attachment with caregivers and reminds kids of their worthiness. Inner child bedtime rituals can do the same for you.

Setting: Your bed (or wherever you sleep).

Objects: A photo of yourself as a small child.

Structure: After your final evening phone scroll, look at the photo, wish them good night and sweet dreams, and tell them you'll be there in the morning when they wake up.

Transition ritual: *Work to Home*

Why it's good: Without an intentional and conscious transition between work and home, our parts can struggle to know how to shift out of work mode. This is especially true if you work from home, where the lines of demarcation between home life and work life are blurry at best.

Setting: If you work from home, do this as soon as you're done with your workday. If you work outside your home, do this ritual as soon as you walk through the door.

Objects: A playlist on your phone and a change of clothes.

Structure: Before you go from answering work emails to folding laundry, take a few minutes to listen to a single song, then change your clothes. Use the same song each time you transition. This ritual helps cue your brain (and your *Go, Fight, Win* parts) that it's time to shift into a different state. If you're an entrepreneur or have any other reason why you must always be in work mode, you can use transition rituals to take short breaks. Even a hastily implemented transition ritual can help your brain feel less saturated.

Transition ritual: *Morning Family Meeting*

Why it's good: Many people roll over and scroll through their phone as soon as they wake up. Others jump out of bed and speed through their task list before the alarm goes off. Both approaches disconnect you from your Self. If you're willing to take a few minutes (or even a few seconds) to check in with your parts, this simple practice can help position you for a more Self-led day.

Setting: Your bed (or wherever you are when you wake up).

Objects: You can use a photo of yourself at any age or an object of your choice to represent your parts.

Structure: Say a quick hello to your mind. Remind all your parts that no matter what happens during your day, *none* of them will be left behind or abandoned by you.

Transition rituals can be helpful any time you want your brain to shift between states. You can do them after a trip, before or after a major event, or when your kids come home from school. Transition rituals are like pressing the clutch on a stick shift—they help you shift smoothly. You can experiment with rituals for both downshifting and upshifting. In the next section, we'll move from transitions to a different kind of connective ritual—celebrations.

Celebration Rituals

Celebrations allow us to mark significant moments, acknowledge achievements, and bring the people we love together. They're supposed to be fun. But somewhere along the way, *celebration* became synonymous with *indulgence*. Celebrations are supposed to make you feel *more* like yourself, not less. When celebrations cause you to make choices you later regret, the activity has ceased to be celebratory and becomes something else entirely.

Why Celebrate?

We often think of celebrations only for special occasions, but just as we expanded the definition of spirituality, we can enlarge the idea of *special* to include all your parts and their efforts to keep you alive. For some people, getting out of pajamas and into the shower *is* a special occasion. So is starting a new job. Or quitting an old one.

Modern Western culture is quick to celebrate relational milestones like weddings and baby showers. But leaving a bad relationship—or choosing to stay single—also deserves "special occasion" status. Inside your mind, there's a big crew of protectors, reactors, and inner children—all of whom deserve recognition. I would be angry and want to quit if I worked a job for decades with no acknowledgment of my efforts. Our parts can feel the same, especially if we consistently ask them to stretch beyond their comfort zones. So let's talk about how you can use celebration rituals to feel more connected. None of these require you to spend money or do any heavy emotional lifting.

Celebration ritual: *Dinner and a Movie*

Why this is good: Breaking bread with other people is a time-honored ritual across cultures. (Adding a movie to the experience is a more modern take.) Because your mind is made of multiple parts, eating solo can be an equally powerful (and often overlooked) ritual. Often we plow through food when we're alone, ignoring the presence of parts. Since you have to eat anyway, why not take the opportunity to include parts work?

Setting: Ideally somewhere with a table or counter. If you don't have one, use your couch or bed. You can do this at home, but for bonus points, take yourself out for a meal.

Objects: A table (if you don't have one, do this wherever you eat), food (no need to cook or do anything showy—this ritual works with a three-course dinner or microwavable mac 'n' cheese), candles, flowers—anything you'd use if you were having a meal with someone very special and important.

Structure: Bust out a nice plate (if you don't have one, you can pick up a beautiful piece of china at a thrift shop), and light the good candle that you've been saving. Take a few minutes before you eat to imagine your parts having a family dinner. Bonus points if you ask them how their day has been; double bonus if you listen to their answer. After you finish your meal, retire to a comfy place and put on a movie, imagining all your parts are there on the couch or in bed with you.

Celebration ritual: *"I Did a Thing" Dance Party*

Why this is good: Dancing is a somatic (body-based) activity that can help reduce stress, improve energy, and release endorphins. You don't need a special occasion, skill, or any other people to do it.

Setting: Wherever you feel most comfortable. You can do a car dance party if you don't have alone time or enough space where you live.

Objects: You, whatever body parts are available to move, and music.

Structure: Set a timer (this can be as short as one minute) and take a deep breath. Before you hit play, tell your parts you're proud of them and that you've chosen to honor their efforts by dancing. Then dance.

Celebration ritual: *Congratulatory Notes*

Why this is good: The act of giving and receiving cards or notes has psychological benefits, including feel-good brain chemicals, a sense of connection, and a feeling that you are valued. When you write *yourself* a note or send yourself a card, your brain doesn't differentiate whether the note came from you or someone else—it still feels good. Sending greeting cards is a centuries-old ritual, one you can harness for the purpose of parts work.

Setting: Wherever you can take a few minutes to write.

Objects: Paper (or a card) and a pen.

Structure: Write yourself a note congratulating yourself for something small. Then mail it. Physical, old-school snail mail is best, but you can also text or email yourself. You can take this ritual into the digital world, too. Sometimes if I'm ordering something from an online source (even if it's something mundane like dog food), I'll fill in the optional gift note with something like "Congratulations, Britt! We're so proud of you!" Silly? Yes—but my brain likes getting notes and doesn't notice or care if I'm the author.

It's good to give your parts recognition for *progress*—not just outcomes. When you choose to celebrate any step forward, even a small one, your parts feel seen and validated. This recognition can boost their morale, encouraging them to repeat whatever behavior you're celebrating. Moreover, celebrations can help your parts feel connected to something greater than themselves, instead of feeling lonely and isolated on an existential island. Celebrations don't lose their power or significance when you do them often—it's not a zero-sum game. Celebrate big things, small things, and everything in between. If for no other reason, do it for the happy juice. When you celebrate, you get a shot of dopamine. This sends the message to your brain, "That was good. Do it again."

Give your parts recognition for *progress*—not just outcomes.

This brings us to our next set of connective rituals—creativity.

Creativity Rituals

Creativity is often thought of as the domain of artists, writers, and musicians, but it is much more than that. Creativity is an essential aspect of human nature that can help you solve problems, increase your confidence, and express your inner world. It also helps with productivity and brain function. Because so many people equate creativity with art, rituals in this area can feel off-putting to people who don't identify as artists. But everyone—including you—is creative. Think about this. How could *anyone* survive infancy, childhood, and adolescence without at least some level of creativity and innovation? Remember, your parts create solutions with or without your input. By consciously choosing to participate in creative rituals, you can better connect with your parts, uncover their hidden talents, and build a deeper sense of Self. The creative rituals here do not require you to sing, paint, or draw anything—and I've made them as vulnerability-free as possible.

Creativity ritual: *Decluttering*
Why this is good: "Clearing" might involve burning palo santo or charging crystals in the moonlight, but it can also mean literally decluttering. Decluttering is an underutilized (and free) ritual. And here's a shocking statistic: "According to researchers at UCLA's Center on Everyday Lives and Families (CELF), clutter has a profound effect on our self-esteem and our moods. A study of thirty-two families found a link between high cortisol (stress hormone) levels of women who had a high density of household objects."*

---

* https://bewell.stanford.edu/a-clean-well-lighted-place/.

When you declutter, your safety parts can relax back, creating more space for your Self to emerge.

Setting: Pick a drawer, a table, a cabinet, a corner of a room, or an entire room.

Objects: Whatever clutter is lying around and two trash bags.

Structure: Set a timer. If you have only two minutes, you can still pick up shoes off the floor or chuck a rogue bag of chips into the trash. Decide which objects to put away, throw away, or donate. Use the two trash bags for donations and trash.

Creativity ritual: *Brainstorm Bad Ideas*

Why this is good: Brainstorming *bad* ideas can be incredibly freeing. It removes the pressure to be perfect and allows your creative parts to play without judgment. This practice can lead to unexpected and surprising solutions, as it encourages out-of-the-box thinking.

Setting: A comfortable and relaxed environment where you won't be interrupted.

Objects: A notebook and pen, or a digital device for note-taking.

Structure: Set a timer for as long or as short as you want, even if it's one minute. Write down the most ridiculous, impractical, and even dangerous ideas you can think of. Because the assignment is to brainstorm bad ideas on purpose, there are no wrong answers. After the timer goes off, review your ideas—you just might find some hidden gems.

> **Brainstorming *bad* ideas can be incredibly freeing.**

Creativity ritual: *Build It*

Why it's good: Building something with your hands can be therapeutic and grounding. Even if you have no sense of your multiplicity, no desire to connect inward, and no experience with therapy, building things is good for your nervous system, since it's a somatic activity and can help with emotional regulation, reduce stress, and even enhance your cognitive functions.

Setting: Anywhere you have space—this can be a table or on the floor.

Objects: Popsicle sticks and glue, Legos, your kids' blocks, or any building materials you prefer.

Structure: Don't worry—the goal here is not to construct the Taj Mahal. In fact, you can trash your creation when you finish. What's most important about this ritual is the act of creating, not the end product. Set a timer (for as many or as few minutes as you want) and use your materials to build whatever you want. There's no right or wrong way to do this—better to create a mess than to create nothing.

Creatrix Madeleine L'Engle, author of *A Wrinkle in Time* and *Walking on Water,* described the importance of creativity best. As she put it:

> But unless we are creators, we are not fully alive. What do I mean by creators? Not only artists, whose acts of creation are the obvious ones of working with paint or clay or words. Creativity is a way of living life, no matter our vocation or how we earn our living. Creativity is not limited to the arts, or having some kind of important career.

A close cousin to creativity, and the subject of our next set of rituals, is play. The word *play* can conjure fear and hesitation in even the most capable and confident adult. Play is often thought of as a frivolous, whipped-cream, nonessential activity. But play is as essential to our well-being as sleep. If I had it my way, every company would have a playground and mandatory recess.

Play Rituals

Play is often associated with childhood, a time when imagination runs wild and every moment is filled with discovery and joy. However, play is not just for kids. It's a fundamental human need that contributes to overall well-being. Play encourages creativity, builds social skills, and enhances resilience. In the context of parts work, play offers a way for our parts to express themselves freely and build a more secure attachment to Self. From the spiritual perspective, play is not just about recreation; it is a vital connective ritual. It allows you to gain clarity and curiosity both inward toward your parts as well as outward, exploring new ideas and possibilities. The barriers to integrating play as an adult are numerous:

Why Adults Don't Play

- *Social stigma:* Some adults may feel embarrassed or self-conscious about engaging in playful activities due to societal expectations or perceptions.
- *Time constraints:* Busy schedules and responsibilities may leave little time for leisure activities, including play.
- *Prioritization of productivity:* Some adults prioritize work and productivity over leisure and play, viewing it as unproductive or unnecessary.
- *Lack of opportunity:* Adults may perceive limited opportunities for play in their environment or may not know how to access playful activities.
- *Stress and burnout:* The last thing we want to do when stressed out is often what we most need—play and rest.

Why They Should

- *Improved mood:* Playing can boost mood and increase feelings of happiness and well-being.

- *Physical health benefits:* Playful activities can contribute to physical health by promoting movement, coordination, and cardiovascular health.
- *Stress relief:* Play provides an outlet for stress and tension, promoting overall well-being and resilience.
- *Increased productivity:* Taking breaks for play can enhance focus, productivity, and overall performance.
- *Improved problem-solving skills:* Playful activities often involve solving problems or overcoming challenges, honing critical thinking skills.

Before we talk about how to incorporate play rituals, let's start with a definition. Things that feel like play for one person (like puzzles) are an anxiety-inducing chore for others (like me). Because we use *play* as a verb (playing a game) but also as a noun (play for play's sake), it can feel confusing. So let's first differentiate *pure play* from *games*—they are not the same.

Pure play: Any activities pursued solely for the sake of enjoying the activity. Pure play includes neither rules nor outcomes.

Games: "The voluntary effort to overcome unnecessary obstacles."* Games have rules and outcomes.

Here's an at-a-glance look at the difference:

	PURE PLAY	GAMES
Definition	Activities purely for enjoyment	Structured activities with rules and objectives
Purpose	Creativity, enjoyment, self-expression	Competition, winning, achieving an outcome

* This definition is courtesy of Bernard Suits in the book *The Grasshopper: Games, Life and Utopia.*

	PURE PLAY	GAMES
Structure	Informal, flexible, no rules, no outcomes, no clear "end"	Defined rules, boundaries, and a clearly defined end with a winner
Examples	Pretend play, imaginative activities, exploration, creativity for creativity's sake	Board games, sports, video games, card games

Adults seem to be better at *games* than *pure play*. This is especially evident if you spend any time observing an eighteen-hole golf course. I've yet to see a recreational adult activity cause as much stress, anxiety, and meltdowns as golf. That's why I appreciate the work of author and golfer Jon Sherman, who encourages players to focus on *enjoying* the game (which has the added benefit of relaxing the body, which helps improve the game). When I asked him why so many adults struggle to play, especially when it comes to golf, he told me, "Every time we play golf, people don't ask, 'Did you have fun?' They ask, 'What did you shoot?' Golf is an extreme example of how we place an emphasis on external results in our society." If you want to flex your play muscles and allow your parts to express themselves, consider trying one of these play rituals:

Play ritual: *Collect an object.*

Why this is good: Nature is good for the soul, the mind, the brain, and every other aspect of our existence. Collecting can be a playful way to feel more mindful and connected to your Self and your parts without any pressure to achieve an outcome. Collecting is a somatic activity that can help your parts slow down and feel safer. It's hard to focus on collecting an object while also running from a lion. The very act of selecting an object has the unintended benefit of cueing safety to protector parts.

Setting: Anywhere outdoors, such as a park, garden, beach, or even your backyard.

Objects: Rocks, leaves, flowers, shells—anything will do. (If you're in a national park or anywhere with signs forbidding the removal of objects, don't do this ritual there.)

Structure: Take a walk outside and look for an object that catches your eye. Spend a few moments appreciating its texture, color, and form. Bring it home and put it in a special place where you can see it often.

Play ritual: *Play catch.*

Why it's good: Playing catch engages multiple cognitive functions simultaneously. It enhances hand-eye coordination, spatial awareness, and motor skills. Additionally, playing catch stimulates the brain's reward system, releasing neurotransmitters like dopamine and endorphins that promote relaxation and positive mood.

Setting: A park, yard, or anywhere inside where you have room to throw something back and forth.

Objects: A ball, a Frisbee, or any nonlethal object that you can easily throw back and forth.

Structure: Find a willing partner and throw the object back and forth. If you don't have someone to play with, you can bounce a ball off a wall. Bonus if you add music.

Play ritual: *Go to a toy store.*

Why this is good: Visiting a toy store can ignite your inner child and spark creativity. It's a chance to explore, play, and experience joy without any agenda. This ritual can help you reconnect with playful parts of yourself that may have been neglected.

Setting: A local toy store or a section of a department store that sells toys.

Objects: Toys and playful items that catch your interest.

Structure: Spend some time browsing the toy store. Allow yourself to play with the toys, try out different games, and reminisce about childhood favorites. You don't have to buy anything. Just enjoy the experience of being surrounded by playful items and letting your imagination run wild.

If you're an adult who struggles with play, don't beat yourself up. Play takes practice—especially if it's been years since you've dusted off a board game or tossed a ball around. If you have critical parts who resist play because it's a "waste of time," remind them of the science. And if you have to trick yourself into playing by thinking of it as a *constructive neural pathway accelerator,* have at it.

Conclusion

Rituals can feel awkward and uncomfortable at first, but eventually they become second nature. Rituals can help maintain balance, predictability, and a sense of order—all of which can help support your brain and nervous system. Humans are inherently rhythmic and cyclical creatures. Practicing your favorite rituals helps anchor you to your *internal* rhythm, so you don't feel as lost trying to find the beat in external things. And whether you decide to build a sandcastle, collect rocks in a jelly jar, or dress up in costume, don't forget to let your parts experiment and play. As you consider your options, ditch the shoulds and take your parts on a field trip they'll *actually* enjoy. And when in doubt, you can always visit your nearest playground—you just might find me and my inner child parts playing on the swings. We'll see you there.

Bottom-Line Takeaways

1. Life is about more than shoulds, oughts, and musts.

2. Spirituality can be thought of simply as connection with yourself and others.

3. Parts work allows you to practice spirituality by connecting inward.

4. It's good to be full of your Self.

5. You don't need to subscribe to a set of beliefs to be spiritual.

6. Rituals can help you connect with your parts.

7. Transition rituals can help your mind switch between states more smoothly.

8. Celebrations aren't about indulging.

9. Creativity is not a synonym for art. You can be creative in any number of forms.

10. Play is a biological necessity, not a luxury.

Action Step Options

I have no time (1–5 minutes):
FIND A SPIRITUAL MOMENT.

For this exercise, you don't have to set aside any time in your day or do anything different. Go about your business, but keep an eye out for flashes, glimmers, or moments when you feel a sense of connection. This can be connection to another person, animal, place, or thing, but if you're able, try to notice a moment of connection with your mind.

I have some time (5–15 minutes):
EXTERNALIZE YOUR PARTS.

Sometimes it can be too crowded and noisy inside your mind to go inside and look around. Externalizing a part of you can help clear space for connection. Choose an object to represent a part of you—it can be any object, and it can be any part. That's it.

Bonus challenge: Imagine what age the part is, what they look like, what they're wearing, and where they live. If you have the time to spare, consider trying to ALIGN with the part: *acknowledge, listen, investigate, give gratitude, negotiate.*

I'll make time (15–45 minutes):
CREATE YOUR OWN RITUALS.

Complete both the above tasks, then either fill in the following charts or copy them into your journal or notebook.

Using the four components of a ritual—intention, setting, objects, structure—create a bespoke transition ritual for yourself. You can use the rituals in this chapter as a guide to get you started, but ultimately decide what transition you want to focus on. Either fill in this chart or copy it into your journal or notebook. You can do this as many times as you want.

Transition Ritual
(how to help your brain shift from one activity to another)

RITUAL ELEMENT	HOW I'M GOING TO DO IT
Intention (*Why am I doing this?*)	
Setting (*Where am I doing this?*)	
Objects (*What will I use?*)	
Structure (*How will I do it?*)	

Celebration Ritual
(to honor one of your parts' process, progress, or outcome)

RITUAL ELEMENT	HOW I'M GOING TO DO IT
Intention (*Why am I doing this?*)	
Setting (*Where am I doing this?*)	
Objects (*What will I use?*)	
Structure (*How will I do it?*)	

Creativity Ritual
(It doesn't have to be art.)

RITUAL ELEMENT	HOW I'M GOING TO DO IT
Intention (*Why am I doing this?*)	
Setting (*Where am I doing this?*)	
Objects (*What will I use?*)	
Structure (*How will I do it?*)	

Play Ritual
(Play is doing something for its own sake.)

RITUAL ELEMENT	HOW I'M GOING TO DO IT
Intention (*Why am I doing this?*)	
Setting (*Where am I doing this?*)	
Objects (*What will I use?*)	
Structure (*How will I do it?*)	

Chapter 9

No Motivation Required

What to Do When You Get Stuck

Within you, there is a stillness and a sanctuary to which you can retreat at anytime and be yourself.
—**Hermann Hesse**

A t the beginning of our adventure together, we talked about my somewhat . . . humble beginnings. I disclosed that at one point, I even found myself alone in a gross bathroom, smoking meth. I'll spare the gory details of that night; suffice it to say, it wasn't a pleasant experience.

But don't worry—you're reading these words, which means circumstances clearly improved. Or as comedian Mike Birbiglia would say, "I'm in the future also."

Now, not everyone has a dramatic "flee the scene" story (I'll tell you how mine ended later in this chapter), but we all know the experience of feeling overwhelmed to the point of total stuckness. Of all the techniques I've ever encountered as both a practicing therapist and a recovering human, parts work was ultimately what alchemized the mess of my former life into the one I enjoy now. Throughout the previous eight chapters, you've learned about fusion—and why separation from your parts is necessary to help them. We've explored the different roles played by different parts, including your inner critic, inner child, and inner indulgers. You've gathered tools like ALIGN and DEFUSE, and we've looked under the hood of your brain's fight/flight/freeze/fawn responses. While every person is different and so is each parts work journey, I've heard the same questions often enough that I want to leave you with an extra toolbox of strategies so you can retrain your relentless inner critic, tend to your terrified inner children when they're frozen and indecisive, and help your indulgent parts *not* go wild on dopamine-seeking binges.

And the best part?

You *don't* need motivation to do any of these exercises. Motivation is an awesome feeling—everyone wants a full tank of "let's do this" energy. But you don't need to feel *anything* to begin to change *everything*. From a neuroscience lens, there's no such thing as an unmotivated person. All your parts have varying motivations and concerns, not all of which are available to your logical and conscious parts. Your brain is *always* motivated, either to make a choice or to survive a threat. By recognizing and acknowledging these conflicting parts, you'll realize resistance and inertia is a *protective mechanism* rather than a lack of motivation. You already have all the motivation you need.

You already have all the motivation you need. That said, here are seven tips and tricks you can use when you feel stuck:

How to Troubleshoot Parts Work

- Do I have to use ALIGN every time a part of me gets triggered?
- I can talk *to* my parts, but I'm having trouble hearing *from* them. Help?
- My mind is too full, and I keep getting distracted. What can I do?

- I've tried to feel my feelings, and it doesn't seem to help at all.
- I don't understand why my parts are triggered.
- How do I manage procrastination?
- What's the number one tool I can use to get myself unstuck?

Do I have to use ALIGN every time a part of me feels triggered?

The ALIGN method (*acknowledge, listen, investigate, give gratitude, negotiate*) is a great way to connect with your parts, but you won't always have the time or the energy to use it. Relationships with partners and close friends don't always require deep-dive conversations. Oftentimes a quick catch-up (or sharing memes or music) is all that's needed to maintain the bond. Developing secure *internal* attachment is the same. While it can be fun to explore the outer reaches of your inner galaxies, if I had to stop and go inside my mind *every* time one of parts felt activated, I would never get anything done. Fortunately, you don't always need to use the ALIGN technique with your parts. Your four other options are to **indulge, distract, ignore,** or **soothe.**

Indulge	Give your part what it wants without seeking to understand or connect with it. This might look like letting yourself have ice cream for breakfast, taking the day off from work, staying in bed, canceling plans, or ordering that random thing off eBay.
Distract	Try to help your part focus on something else besides its concern. Watch a movie, crochet a dinosaur, scroll online, or go out and do anything to distract your mind. This doesn't always work (especially if a part is activated higher than a 5 on a scale of 1 to 10), but it is always an option on the menu.

Ignore	*Sometimes* you can get away with ignoring your parts, though if you have a habit of ignoring yourself, ignoring isn't a great option (nor will it be effective). Once you build a solid relationship with your parts, it'll become easier to ignore them occasionally without rupturing your bond.
Soothe	Soothing is focusing on symptom management instead of problem resolution. This is a totally valid approach. Soothing a part might look like taking medication, using weighted blankets or sensory tools, or avoiding triggers.

How will I know which one to do?

Think of your physical body—not every bump, scrape, ache, or twitch requires you to stop and pay attention to it or intervene. The same is true with your parts. The trick is to know which approach to take and when to use it. Think of the indulge/distract/ignore/soothe options like parenting strategies.

Indulge: It's not healthy to always give in, but sometimes (especially when life kicks you in the face) it's easier to give the kids extra screen time and call it a day. The same is true for your parts.

Distract: If your dog starts eating your shoes, it's helpful to distract them with something more appropriate. When a part of you is focused on something unhelpful or harmful, try to redirect your attention to something more constructive. This strategy is the equivalent of giving your mind a chew toy.

Ignore: It would be profoundly unkind to habitually ignore a child, but sometimes minor complaints resolve themselves on their own. By not giving attention to certain feelings or thoughts, you're removing the reinforcement (attention) that keeps them active. In behavioral psychology, this approach is known as *extinguishing*.

Soothe: Soothing involves providing comfort and care to your parts when they are distressed or in need of attention. But be careful with this option. Too much soothing can prohibit growth and resilience. It's important for children (and your parts) to learn to cope with challenges and to tolerate distress. Triggers aren't inherently bad; they're storytellers with important information to share. If you've forgotten entire chunks of your life, triggers can help you piece together the puzzle of your past.

As you practice connecting with parts, it will get easier to know which of the four choices will be best suited for a particular occasion.

I can talk to my parts, but I'm having trouble hearing from them. Help?

When you first start noticing your parts, it can feel easier to talk *at* rather than listen *to* them. As is true with any relationship, parts work requires two-way communication. But the idea of talking and listening to parts is a different way to think about thinking. We're used to talking to ourselves in *first person* (*I* feel . . . , *My* triggers are . . . , It bothers *me* when . . .). But first-person self-talk creates a state of fusion where there's no separation between your Self and your parts.

To help solve this problem, you can think of your inner conversations as an inner *dialogue* versus an inner *monologue*. Inner dialogue is a switch from first-person (*I, me, my* . . .) to third-person self-talk using your name or pronouns (*Britt* feels . . . , *Her* triggers are . . . , *She* feels sad when . . .). This switch from first-person to third-person self-talk, known as illeism, changes your thinking from an inner monologue to an inner dialogue. Most people are kinder to other people than they are to themselves, and third-person self-talk allows you to direct the same compassion and comfort you'd give a friend inward toward your parts.

Changing your inner monologue to a dialogue feels weird when you first try it, but science backs this practice up. Third-person self-talk slows your brain down and creates space between a stimulus and your response,* so you can be responsive instead of reactive. I'll give you three ways you can create an inner dialogue—the coffee cup solution, chair work, and an exercise called "externalizing the part." These techniques can feel intense, so if at any point you become flooded, overwhelmed, or unsafe, immediately stop. It's best to practice these techniques using non-trauma-related situations. If your situation feels higher than a 5 on an intensity scale of 1 to 10, consider trying these techniques with a trauma-trained therapist, coach, or counselor if that's an option.

The Coffee Cup Solution
(Based on the Jungian Principle of Active Imagination)

Either first thing in the morning or at the end of the day, grab two coffee cups (or whatever drinking vessel suits your lifestyle), and fill them both with a beverage of your choice. Sit down with one cup either next to or across from the other cup. Then imagine you're sitting with one of your parts. Have a conversation out loud, asking questions about their feelings and needs, listening for their responses, and talking with them as you would a friend. You can do this silently, but it works best out loud. You will feel uneasy doing this— but it works.

---

* As Viktor Frankl put it, "Between stimulus and response there is a space. In that space is our power to choose our response. In our response lies our growth and our freedom."

Chair Work
(Adapted from Gestalt Therapy, Originated by Fritz Perls)

Chair work is a powerful technique used in parts therapy to facilitate a dialogue between different aspects of yourself. It helps you externalize and interact with your parts in a physical space, making the process more tangible and effective.

How to Do It

1. **Set up your space:** Find a quiet room with two chairs. Place them facing each other. Label one chair as Self and the other as Part (e.g., Angry Part, Sad Part, Anxious Part).

2. **Identify the part:** Choose a part you want to work with. This could be a part that's currently distressing you or one you want to understand better.

3. **Take a seat:** Sit in the Self chair and ground yourself. Take a few deep breaths and make sure you feel curious and open toward the part. (If you're angry with or afraid of the part, that's a sign you're fused and might need to DEFUSE first.)

4. **Switch chairs:** Move to the Part chair and embody that part. Speak from the perspective of the part, expressing its feelings, thoughts, and needs. For example, if you're working with your Angry Part, say, "I feel so angry because . . ."

5. **Dialogue:** Switch back to the Self chair and respond to the part. Ask questions to understand it better, offer comfort, and discuss possible solutions. Continue switching chairs and maintaining the dialogue until you feel a sense of resolution or understanding.

6. **Reflection:** After the exercise, reflect on the experience. Write down any insights, feelings, or actions you want to take based on the dialogue.

Externalizing the Part
(*A Technique Used in Directive Play Therapy*)

Externalizing your parts using a physical object can help make your inner dialogues more concrete. This technique allows you to project your parts onto an object, making it easier to interact with them.

How to Do It

1. **Choose an object:** Select an object that can represent your part. This could be a stuffed animal, a toy, a pillow, or any other item that you feel comfortable using.

2. **Identify the part:** Decide which part you want to work with. This could be a part that is currently causing you distress or one that you want to understand better.

3. **Set the scene:** Find a quiet, comfortable place to sit. Place the chosen object in front of you and take a few deep breaths. Make sure you feel curious toward and open to the part.

4. **Project the part:** Imagine that the object represents the part you want to engage with. Visualize this part's emotions, thoughts, and characteristics being embodied by the object.

5. **Initiate the dialogue:** Begin talking to the object as if it were the part. Ask it questions about how it feels, what it needs, and what it wants you to understand. Speak to it with the same compassion and curiosity you would offer a friend.

6. **Listen for responses:** After asking a question, pause and listen for any responses that come to mind. This might feel like an inner voice, a thought, or an intuition. Speak these responses out loud, as if the object is talking back to you.

7. **Continue the conversation:** Maintain the dialogue, alternating between asking questions and listening to the part's responses. Explore its feelings, its needs, and any messages it has for you.

8. **Conclude and reflect:** When you feel the conversation has reached a natural conclusion, thank the part for sharing with you. Take a moment to reflect on the experience and any insights gained. You might jot down a few notes if that feels helpful, but it's not necessary.

This exercise of externalizing the part with an object helps create a clear distinction between your Self and your parts, making the inner dialogue more tangible and effective. By engaging in this compassionate conversation, you can better understand and address the needs of your parts.

My mind is too full, and I keep getting distracted. What can I do?

When your mind is too busy with tasks, worries, and a never-ending to-do list, trying to do parts work in your head or even out loud can be difficult. To help move through this type of stuckness, I'll give you two different options to try.

Option One:
Nondominant Writing

Nondominant writing involves using your opposite hand to write a letter from your parts to your Self. This technique

allows your parts to communicate their previously unconscious thoughts and feelings and was popularized by art
therapist and author Dr. Lucia Capacchione in her book *The
Power of Your Other Hand.*

When you write with your nondominant hand, you deactivate your brain's autopilot setting and access previously
unconscious thoughts and feelings. This exercise may feel
uncomfortable and strange at first, so make sure you have
uninterrupted time and space. Start by thinking of which
part you want to invite into the conversation. Then in your
notebook or journal, use your opposite hand to free-write
from the part's point of view for a set time (you can go for as
little as thirty seconds or for as long as you want). Five to ten
minutes is usually enough to get past the initial awkward-
ness of the exercise. You'll probably feel silly and wonder if
you're making things up. You're not.

Example: Let's say I notice what feels like an angry teenage part. I'll sit down and say (out loud) to this part, "I want
to know what you're going through. Please take this pen
and write me a letter and say anything you want to say. I
won't get mad at you or yell at you." Then with my right
hand (normally I'm left-handed), I let her write whatever she
needs to say onto the page. To close out the exercise, I'll read
the letter out loud to myself and then say, "Thank you for
sharing this with me."

Option Two:
Drawing Your Parts

Materials Needed:

- ☐ Paper
- ☐ Colored pencils, markers, or crayons

How to Do It

- **Set the scene:** Find a quiet, comfortable space where you can focus on the activity without interruptions.
- **Identify your parts:** Take a moment to think about the different parts of yourself you want to explore. These could be parts that represent various emotions, roles, or aspects of your personality (e.g., the inner critic, the nurturer, the playful child).
- **Draw your parts:** On a piece of paper, draw each part as a separate figure or symbol. Don't worry about artistic skill; the focus is on expression, not on perfection. Use different colors and shapes to represent each part's unique characteristics and emotions.
- **Label the parts:** Give each drawing a name or a label that represents the part it depicts (e.g., Angry Part, Sad Part, Protective Part).
- **Dialogue with your parts:** After drawing, take a few moments to reflect on each part. You can write a brief description next to each drawing about how that part feels, what it wants, and what it needs. Alternatively, you can have a verbal dialogue with your drawings, asking questions and responding as if the drawings are speaking back to you.
- **Reflect on the Self:** Draw a representation of your Self, distinct from the parts. This can be a figure or a symbol that embodies your core self, the part of you that is observing and compassionate. Place this drawing in the center of the page or on a separate sheet.
- **Arrange and reflect:** Arrange your drawings in a way that makes sense to you. This might be in a circle around the Self, in a line, or in any configuration that feels right. Reflect on the relationships between your Self and your parts. Notice any patterns, connections, or conflicts.

These exercises are uncomfortable, sort of like the psychological equivalent of burpees, but they do help to differentiate your Self from your parts, clearing the way for authentic connection.

I've tried to feel my feelings, and it doesn't seem to help at all.

When you're flooded *by* your feelings, that's not the same as defusing from and being *with* your feelings. When you're fused, there is no distinction between your Self and the parts, so feelings tend to build up in big waves, crash down on your head, then recede and return. Being *with* your feelings means acknowledging them and allowing them to exist **without letting them take over**. When you can hold space for the feelings *alongside* your parts, not *as* your parts, you maintain a sense of Self while also attending to the needs of the part.

If you struggle to create enough separation to align with your parts, practice using all the DEFUSE elements *except the F* (feelings) until you feel your body come into a state of regulation. You'll know you're there when you feel curious and open toward your parts* instead of punched in the gut by their feelings.

D: Describe your sensations.

E: Exit the room.

F: Feel your feelings.

U: Use your senses.

S: Shift your body.

E: Exhale.

---

* Assessing your feelings of openness and curiosity toward your parts is a technique from Internal Family Systems.

I don't understand why my parts are triggered.

As a therapist, I've made a career out of understanding why people do, think, and feel the things they do. Analyzing behavior, observing patterns, and uncovering origin stories is often useful. For many people, understanding the genesis of our struggles is necessary to break free. But here's a surprising strategy when you get stuck in analysis land. *Don't* start with why.

Don't Start with Why

If you're familiar with the work of Simon Sinek, his book *Start with Why* is the gold standard in the business world. Finding your why is a genius business strategy, but it doesn't translate to personal stuckness. When you're fused with parts, flooded by feelings, or trying to get unstuck from long-standing habits or patterns, why questions often make things worse.

You wouldn't walk up to a burning building and say, "Hmm, I wonder why this building is on fire." Figuring out why the building caught on fire is important, but the first order of business is to get the people out. When you're besieged by anxiety, stress, or burnout, asking, "Why do I feel like this?" is *not* helpful at the starting gate. Instead, a better question is "What are three people, places, thoughts, or things I can choose right now to help me keep moving forward?"

This brings us to our next FAQ, the source of many battles, many shame storms, and much confusion—procrastination.

How do I manage procrastination?

Procrastination is not a character defect or a sign that you're unmotivated. As I said at the beginning of this chapter, there's no such thing as being "unmotivated"—your brain is always motivated. Sometimes your safety teams' efforts to preserve life take higher priority than your logical parts' desire to achieve goals. Procrastination is not self-sabotage—it's self-protection. From the parts work lens, procrastination is an example of *polarization*, which we discussed in chapter 5. One part of you believes that the best way to survive is to do the task, while another part insists that *not* doing it is the better option. These opposing positions create a freeze response, which is why procrastination isn't a mental challenge but a physical one. To complicate matters, procrastination also comes with a slew of benefits.

How Can Procrastinating Be Beneficial?

Procrastination has its perks—it can preserve your image, prevent you from failing, and give you a massive drug hit. Until I learned about the brain, I didn't realize the adrenaline and dopamine rush from racing against the clock becomes its own addictive cycle. *When the Body Says No* author and addiction expert Gabor Maté put it this way:

> *For those habituated to high levels of internal stress since early childhood, it is the absence of stress that creates unease, evoking boredom and a sense of meaninglessness. People may become addicted to their own stress hormones, adrenaline and cortisol.*

When you understand the *function* of a behavior, it can be easier to sustainably change it. We get stuck with procrastination not because of our personality traits, but because of our *physiological states*. Procrastination is a manifestation of anxiety that gets mislabeled as laziness. You're not lazy or unmotivated, but your brain's definition of motivation will differ from yours if it perceives a threat.

What's the number one tool I can use to get myself unstuck?

In the nineties movie *Entrapment*, there's an amazing scene where an art thief (played by the gorgeous Catherine Zeta-Jones) attempts a heist by carefully maneuvering through a room guarded by laser beams. (Tom Cruise's character Ethan Hunt pulls off a similar feat in the *Mission Impossible* vault scene.) Your mind, much like the laser-protected rooms in those movies, is also armed with a security system—one that's highly intricate and sensitive to movement. But there's one tool you can use to maneuver around your mind without tripping your brain's alarm, scaring your protectors, or causing your inner critic to shut you down. This tool works whether your challenge is starting a business, changing a habit, feeling less anxious, or leaving a relationship.

I call it the *micro-yes*.

A micro-yes is the smallest possible thing you can say yes to *right now*. Not next week, not tomorrow, not after you finish the "bad food,"* and not after you sober up. A micro-yes is smaller than a small step, and it's smaller than a baby step. A micro-yes is the tiniest action you can take without your brain's security guards rushing to your rescue. The best way to illustrate the power of the micro-yes is to return to that bathroom on the final night I smoked meth.

Here's what happened next. . . .

As I looked around the bathroom and saw the rusty tub, cracked mirror, and empty drug baggies, I heard a voice in my head kindly but firmly say, *No one is coming to save you, and there's no one left to blame. No more excuses, Britt. This is **your** problem.* . . . I took the hit, put the pipe down on the sink, and walked out the door. When I got myself to a

---

* There's no "bad food." There's also no "clean food"—all food is clean unless you drop it on the floor.

safe place, you'd think I'd have felt relieved. But I wasn't just walking out on a drug habit—I was walking out on an entire life and leaving behind everything and everyone I had known. I was also tweaking (a delightful combination of hyperactivity, paranoia, and insomnia). So I did the only thing I could think of in that moment—I called a friend.

When she answered the phone, I told her *everything*. Between my ugly crying and nonsensical rambling, I also ambushed her with every question whizzing around my mind:

- Why did I *do* this to myself?
- What's *wrong* with me?
- How did I let things get *this* bad?
- What am I going to do?

And she listened patiently for a while, then said the most insightful, powerful, and significant sentence anyone could possibly have uttered in that moment: "Um, Britt, when was the last time you ate food?"

Oh yeah. Food.

The truth was, I had been so wrapped up trying to maintain my double life, I had neglected the most basic of human needs. I couldn't remember the last time I had eaten anything except meth dust.

She patiently said, "Okay, Britt, can you go to your fridge?"

And I said yes.

She said, "Can you open it up and find something in there to eat?"

I opened the fridge and found a single yogurt hiding in the back. I grabbed the yogurt and proudly said, "*Yes!*"

"Have you got a spoon?"

And that woman sat with me on the phone, spoonful by spoonful, micro-yes by micro-yes, for an *entire hour*. By giving me a series of small things to say yes to, she was helping my brain shift from overwhelm to action. From analysis to decisiveness. From stuck to unstuck.

And here's the beauty of the micro-yeses: you don't need a catastrophic event to benefit from doing them. Your micro-yes is waiting for you *right now*, and it wants to drive you to your next destination—even if you don't know exactly where that is. When I was in that bathroom feeling broken, feeling like change was *not* possible, feeling so far away from the person I wanted to be, I had no idea that such small yeses would lead to such big changes. But I went from that life to this one by saying yes. And then doing it again. And then doing it again.

> **Your micro-yes is waiting for you *right now*.**

Micro-yeses are so easy, it almost feels ridiculous to do them. But remember how brains are designed: they don't like change, and they can easily get indigestion if you try to take bites that are too big. Even if you don't think a step should feel big, your brain gets to decide. If you think a step is small and you're not doing it, that's likely because it isn't small enough. A micro-yes is the smallest step you can think of cut up in to a dozen pieces. Here are some practical non-drug-related examples:

THE CHALLENGE	A BABY STEP	A MICRO-YES
Starting a fitness routine	Go for a walk around the block after work.	Put your left sneaker by the door. Then go back to the couch.
Getting your finances in order	Do a budget.	Download a budget app or open a spreadsheet, but don't do anything else.
Starting a business	Write a business plan.	Make a note to yourself to write a business plan.

THE CHALLENGE	A BABY STEP	A MICRO-YES
Answering an email	Draft the email.	Start a new email but fill in only the subject line.
Decluttering	Set a timer for 30 minutes and clean one corner of a room.	Pick one thing up off the floor.

Micro-yeses allow you to maneuver under the laser beams of your brain without getting stuck.

How am I supposed to get anywhere if I'm taking steps this small?

You'll move forward faster doing micro-yeses than by taking big steps, getting stuck, feeling shame, and then repeating the cycle. And remember, the pace you start at is *not* the pace you stay at. Even the smallest yes sets off a chain reaction in your brain, and then it rapidly compounds, and suddenly you're able to go farther faster and sustain your momentum. Micro-yeses release microdoses of dopamine, which helps you build the habit of repeating them.*

The pace you start at is *not* the pace you stay at.

It can be tempting to analyze the why. To be sure, clarity and understanding are important. I've dedicated my career to that process. But *insight* doesn't equal *action*. You can have all the insight in the world and still feel stuck. Information becomes *transformation* the second you say yes to anything, no matter how small.

At the beginning of our journey, I asked you to imagine if all the voices in your head could get along. But here's a surprising truth—*they don't need to.*

---

* Micro-yeses won't work if you beat yourself up for doing only small things. You need to acknowledge the small win to bank its benefit.

As the leader of the boardroom inside your head, you don't need to wait for everyone to feel inspired, to agree, or to feel ready. As we said in the introduction, you don't need readiness, only *willingness*. Willingness to say yes to whatever it takes—*as small as it takes.*

You don't need readiness, only willingness.

So, what's your first micro-yes going to be?

You might decide to compose the text, buy the floss, or order the deluxe Crayola set. It's fun to dream about results, because that's where you'll usually find the cheering crowds and social-media-worthy photo opportunities. But solving for the starting gate is a better use of our energy than fantasizing about the finish line. Micro-yeses don't look like much, but they *do* get you out of the gap between a good intention and a successful outcome. Micro-yeses build momentum. No motivation required.

So instead of fighting with your mind, give it what it needs:

Small yeses.

Every day.

Starting now.

Final Thoughts

I used to think there was an ultimate level of psychological health, one where the head chatter would quiet down and I wouldn't feel so fragmented. But when I learned about the multidimensional nature of the human mind, suddenly an expansive inner world opened up, one where all my parts could peacefully coexist. This experience is available to you, too.

Instead of thinking of yourself as a good person or a bad person, imagine if there was room at the table for you to be kind, jealous, loving, anxious, joyful, cranky, and everything in between. The more access we have to our parts, the better our lives work and the more we feel a sense of ease and flow. **The art of inner healing is not to erase your parts—it's to understand them.** With Self at the center of the system, fully in awe of and in love with its parts, we create the space necessary for these messy, magical lives.

Ironically, if we want to integrate, we need to separate. I call this the paradox of wholeness, the strange situation whereby wholeness requires *more* connection to our multiplicity, not less. **Wholeness is not the absence of parts. It's the presence of Self alongside the parts.**

Think of this like the concept of whole foods in nutrition.

Wholeness is not the absence of parts. It's the presence of Self alongside the parts.

Whole foods are unprocessed foods* with nothing added and nothing removed. Processed food can include things like synthetic dyes and artificial sweeteners, while important nutrients (like fiber) are often removed. The same is true for our personalities. To feel whole, we don't want unnatural additives (like the *shoulds*, *oughts*, and *musts*), and we don't want to take anything away, since even the shadowy side of your personality has nutritional value.

Parts work isn't about being more productive—though you likely will be. And it isn't about finding happiness—though that's a common by-product. Parts work won't necessarily make your life easier or help you bypass pain, but it can strengthen your capacity to cope with the madness of modern life—especially in your relationships. Parts work allows us to not only see ourselves clearly but also have more kindess and tolerance toward other people—even the ones we don't understand. As Dr. Richard Schwartz put it, "If people could see themselves and each other and know the presence of both ours and others' internal protectors that are operating, we would have a lot more compassion and respect for each other."

My greatest wish in writing this book is for you to *stop* thinking of your mind as the enemy. Your brain is on your side—it always has been. And when you sit with your parts around the campfire and listen to their stories, you'll realize you're not alone—and you never will be. When you know who you are and what you're made of, and you start to see that all your parts have value, suddenly you're doing things you never thought possible.

You have a vast universe inside your mind, filled with surprises and adventures. And you have an entire star system of parts, hoping you'll come find them and bring them home.

Let's go get them.

---

* Processed foods are not necessarily bad, and for some people they are the only accessible and affordable option.

Acknowledgments

I am extraordinarily grateful to Dr. Richard Schwartz for gifting the world with the Internal Family Systems model and for so generously supporting its practitioners. Big thank-you to my superhero literary agent, Rachel Beck at Liza Dawson Associates, for leading me on our third trip through book Wonderland. There aren't enough words to adequately express my gratitude to Marian Lizzi and the team at TarcherPerigee and Penguin Random House for believing in me and my work. To my friends who held space, offered ideas, and read pages—Jenn Berry, Ally Bogard, Vanessa Cornell, Crystle Lampitt, Dr. Joy Erlichman Miller, Amber Rae, Nicole Whiting—THANK YOU.

Gratitude to my circus coaches, Kelsey Aicher and Elena Sherman, for their wisdom, patience, and support on my aerial journey—and for allowing me to use their words and stories in these pages. Thank you to Deborah Hanekamp and Jon Sherman for your contributions to the world. Thank you to Ryan Estis for providing the feedback that inspired the title of this book and to Danielle Ross for story-crafting wizardry. Grateful to the sparkly powerhouse Laura Gassner Otting for penning the foreword. To all my clients past, present, and future—thank you for allowing me to witness your parts. Thank you to my therapist, Bob Falconer, for never letting my therapist parts take over during sessions and for creating a safe space to do hard things.

And finally, to my husband, Michael—thank you for being an exceptional partner to me and all my parts (and for being the best dog dad to Oscar). I appreciate, respect, and love you.

Suggested Reading

Marina Abramović and Jeannette Fischer. *Psychoanalyst Meets Marina Abramović: Artist Meets Jeannette Fischer.* Scheidegger and Spiess, 2018.

Becky A. Bailey. *I Love You Rituals.* William Morrow Paperbacks, 2000.

Ally Bogard. *The Quiet Teachers: Becoming a Student of Your Life.* Parea Books, 2024.

John Bradshaw. *Homecoming: Reclaiming and Championing Your Inner Child.* Bantam, 1990.

Lucia Capacchione. *Recovery of Your Inner Child.* Touchstone, 1991.

Rita Carter. *Multiplicity: The New Science of Personality, Identity, and the Self.* Little, Brown Spark, 2008.

Mihaly Csikszentmihalyi. *Flow: The Psychology of Optimal Experience.* Harper Perennial, 2016.

Dalai Lama XIV et al. *A Policy of Kindness: An Anthology of Writings by and About the Dalai Lama.* Snow Lion, 1993.

Ralph De La Rosa and Richard Schwartz. *Outshining Trauma: A New Vision of Radical Self-Compassion Integrating*

Internal Family Systems and Buddhist Meditation. Shambhala, 2024.

Jay Earley. *Self-Therapy: A Step-by-Step Guide to Creating Wholeness Using IFS, a Cutting-Edge Psychotherapy,* 3rd ed. Pattern System Books, 2022.

Clarissa Pinkola Estés. *Women Who Run with the Wolves: Myths and Stories of the Wild Woman Archetype.* Ballantine Books, 1995.

James Fadiman and Jordan Gruber. *Your Symphony of Selves: Discover and Understand More of Who We Are.* Park Street Press, 2020.

Robert Falconer. *The Others Within Us: Internal Family Systems, Porous Mind, and Spirit Possession.* Great Mystery Press, 2023.

Roger Fisher and William Ury. *Getting to Yes: Negotiating Agreement Without Giving In,* 3rd ed., Penguin Books, 2011.

Elizabeth Gilbert. *Big Magic: Creative Living Beyond Fear.* New York: Riverhead Books, 2015.

Regina A. Goulding and Richard C. Schwartz. *The Mosaic Mind: Empowering the Tormented Selves of Child Abuse Survivors.* Trailheads Publications, 2003.

Harville Hendrix. *Getting the Love You Want: A Guide for Couples.* St. Martin's Griffin, 2019.

Toni Herbine-Blank and Martha Sweezy. *Internal Family Systems Couple Therapy Skills Manual: Healing Relationships with Intimacy from the Inside Out.* PESI, 2021.

Jeremy Holmes. *John Bowlby and Attachment Theory,* 2nd ed. Routledge, 2014.

Robert A. Johnson. *Owning Your Own Shadow: Understanding the Dark Side of the Psyche.* HarperSanFrancisco, 1994.

Ethan Kross. *Chatter.* Crown, 2021.

Mike Krzyzewski. *Leading with the Heart: Coach K's Successful Strategies for Basketball, Business, and Life.* Grand Central, 2023.

John Lee. *Growing Yourself Back Up: Understanding Emotional Regression.* Harmony, 2001.

Amir Levine and Rachel Heller. *Attached: The New Science of Adult Attachment and How It Can Help You Find—and Keep—Love.* TarcherPerigee, 2012.

Peter Levine. *Trauma and Memory: Brain and Body in a Search for the Living Past.* North Atlantic Books, 2015.

———. *Waking the Tiger: Healing Trauma.* North Atlantic Books, 1997.

Marc Lewis. *The Biology of Desire: Why Addiction Is Not a Disease.* Scribe Publications, 2016.

Marsha M. Linehan. *DBT Skills Training Manual,* 2nd ed. Guilford Press, 2015.

Gabor Maté. *In the Realm of Hungry Ghosts.* North Atlantic Books, 2010.

Kelly McDaniel. *Mother Hunger: How Adult Daughters Can Understand and Heal from Lost Nurturance, Protection, and Guidance.* Hay House, 2021.

David McRaney. *How Minds Change: The Surprising Science of Belief, Opinion, and Persuasion.* Portfolio, 2022.

Pia Mellody. *Facing Codependence: What It Is, Where It Comes From, How It Sabotages Our Lives.* Harper & Row, 2003.

Jay S. Noricks. *Parts Psychology: A New Model of Therapy for the Treatment of Psychological Problems Through Healing the Normal Multiple Personalities Within Us.* New University Press, 2011.

John O'Donohue. *Anam Cara: A Book of Celtic Wisdom.* Harper Perennial, 1997.

Laura Gassner Otting. *Wonderhell: Why Success Doesn't Feel Like It Should . . . and What to Do About It.* Ideapress, 2024.

Vienna Pharaon. *The Origins of You: How Breaking Family Patterns Can Liberate the Way We Live and Love.* G. P. Putnam's Sons, 2023.

John K. Pollard III, *Self-Parenting: The Complete Guide to Your Inner Conversations.* Self-Parenting Program, 1987.

Stephen W. Porges. *The Pocket Guide to the Polyvagal Theory: The Transformative Power of Feeling Safe.* W. W. Norton, 2017.

Amber Rae. *Choose Wonder over Worry: Move Beyond Fear and Doubt to Unlock Your Full Potential.* St. Martin's Essentials, 2020.

David Rock. *Your Brain at Work: Strategies for Overcoming Distraction, Regaining Focus, and Working Smarter All Day Long.* HarperBusiness, 2009.

John Rowan. *Subpersonalities: The People Inside Us.* Routledge, 1990.

Richard C. Schwartz. *Introduction to Internal Family Systems.* Sounds True, 2023.

———. *No Bad Parts: Healing Trauma and Restoring Wholeness with the Internal Family Systems Model.* Sounds True, 2021.

———. *You Are the One You've Been Waiting For: Applying*

Internal Family Systems to Intimate Relationships. Sounds True, 2023.

Richard C. Schwartz and Robert R. Falconer. *Many Minds, One Self: Evidence for a Radical Shift in Paradigm.* Trailheads Center for Self Leadership, 2017.

Jon Sherman. *The Four Foundations of Golf: How to Build a Game That Lasts a Lifetime.* Practical Golf, 2022.

Daniel J. Siegel. *Aware: The Science and Practice of Presence.* TarcherPerigee, 2020.

———. *Mindsight: The New Science of Personal Transformation.* Bantam, 2010.

Martha Sweezy and Ellen L. Ziskind, eds. *Internal Family Systems Therapy: New Dimensions.* Routledge, 2013.

Stan Tatkin. *Wired for Love: How Understanding Your Partner's Brain and Attachment Style Can Help You Defuse Conflict and Build a Secure Relationship.* New Harbinger Publications, 2011.

Nedra Glover Tawwab. *Set Boundaries, Find Peace: A Guide to Reclaiming Yourself.* TarcherPerigee, 2021.

Bessel A. van der Kolk. *The Body Keeps the Score: Brain, Mind, and Body in the Healing of Trauma.* Penguin, 2015.

Alan Watts. *Become What You Are.* Shambhala, 2003.

Stephen Wolinsky. *The Dark Side of the Inner Child: The Next Step.* Bramble Books, 1993.

Dimitris Xygalatas. *Ritual: How Seemingly Senseless Acts Make Life Worth Living.* Little, Brown Spark, 2022.

Connie Zweig and Steve Wolf. *Romancing the Shadow: A Guide to Soul Work for a Vital, Authentic Life.* Wellspring/ Ballantine Books, 1999.

Index

About the Author

Britt Frank, LSCSW, SEP, is a licensed neuropsychotherapist, keynote speaker, and author of *The Getting Unstuck Workbook* and *The Science of Stuck*, named by the Society for Human Resource Management, *Esquire*, *New York*, and the Next Big Idea Club as a must-read. Britt received her undergraduate degree from Duke University and her master's degree from the University of Kansas, where she later became an award-winning adjunct instructor. She is a contributing writer to *Psychology Today*, and her work has been featured in *The New York Times*, *Forbes*, *Self*, and *Fast Company*, and on NPR, Psych Central, and Thrive Global. Britt speaks and writes widely about emotional wellness and personal leadership.

ALSO BY
BRITT FRANK

Tarcher